MULTIMOD Mark III
The Core Dynamic and Steady-State Models

Douglas Laxton, Peter Isard,
Hamid Faruqee, Eswar Prasad, and Bart Turtelboom

INTERNATIONAL MONETARY FUND
Washington DC
May 1998

Cover design, charts, and composition:
Theodore F. Peters Jr., Choon Lee, and IMF Graphics Section

Library of Congress Cataloging-in-Publication Data

MULTIMOD Mark III : the core dynamic and steady-state models /
  Douglas Laxton . . . [et al.]. — Washington, DC : International
Monetary Fund, [1998].
      p.   cm. — (Occasional paper, ISSN 0251-6365 ; no. 164)

    Includes bibliographical references.
    ISBN 1-55775-722-4

    1. Econometric models. 2. Economic forecasting — Econometric
models. 3. Economic policy — Econometric models. 4. International
finance — Econometric models. 5. Macroeconomics — Econometric
models — Evaluation. I. Laxton, Douglas. II. Series: Occasional paper
(International Monetary Fund) ; no. 164.
    HB141.M84 1998

Price: US$18.00
(US$15.00 to full-time faculty members and
students at universities and colleges)

Please send orders to:
International Monetary Fund, Publication Services
700 19th Street, N.W., Washington, D.C. 20431, U.S.A.
Tel.: (202) 623-7430   Telefax: (202) 623-7201
E-mail: publications@imf.org
Internet: http://www.imf.org

recycled paper

Contents

CONTENTS

Tables

Section

Box

Figures

Section

Box

The following symbols have been used throughout this paper:

. . . to indicate that data are not available;

n.a. to indicate not applicable;

— to indicate that the figure is zero or less than half the final digit shown, or that the item does not exist;

– between years or months (e.g., 1994–95 or January–June) to indicate the years or months covered, including the beginning and ending years or months;

/ between years (e.g., 1994/95) to indicate a crop or fiscal (financial) year.

"Billion" means a thousand million.

Minor discrepancies between constituent figures and totals are due to rounding.

The term "country," as used in this paper, does not in all cases refer to a territorial entity that is a state as understood by international law and practice; the term also covers some territorial entities that are not states, but for which statistical data are maintained and provided internationally on a separate and independent basis.

Preface

This study, prepared in the Economic Modeling and External Adjustment Division (EMEAD) of the Research Department, describes the Mark III version of MULTI-MOD, the IMF's multiregion macroeconometric model. The development of MULTI-MOD Mark III resulted from a major effort during 1997 to incorporate several basic changes into the Mark II version. Douglas Laxton, senior economist, took command of the project and is largely responsible for the work that has been done. Peter Isard, Division Chief, interacted closely with Laxton, both in the ongoing decision-making process that accompanied the technical work and in managing the preparation of this paper. Hamid Faruqee was integrally involved in developing the analytic framework that underpins the new specification of consumption and saving behavior, and in drafting Section V. Bart Turtelboom contributed significantly to the development of the investment equations and prepared Section VI. Eswar Prasad prepared Sections VII and VIII.

The Mark III version retains many of the features of earlier versions of MULTI-MOD. It thus reflects substantial past work on the Mark II version by Paul Masson, Steven Symansky, and Guy Meredith, and on the Mark I version by Masson, Symansky, Richard Haas, and Michael Dooley. As Deputy Division Chief of EMEAD from 1987 to November 1995, Symansky also contributed to a series of refinements of the core Mark II model, along with the development of several extended versions of the Mark II model. Similarly, Meredith continued to work on MULTIMOD after completion of the initial version of Mark II, contributing to the foundations for the Mark III investment function. Masson and Meredith provided numerous constructive comments on an initial draft of this study, as did Peter Clark and Thomas Krueger.

To an important extent, the conceptual improvements in the Mark III version reflect feedback from users outside the IMF. We are particularly grateful for comments and encouragement received from Ralph Bryant, John Helliwell, and Assaf Razin. Others outside the IMF have contributed importantly in more technical ways. We thank Richard Black for help with programming the macro used to derive the steady-state analogue model; Michel Juillard and Peter Hollinger for their efforts in developing a reliable solution algorithm for solving forward-looking models; Hope Pioro for general programming assistance and help in creating the computer modeling system; and Irene Chan for work on the database.

Within the IMF, the construction of the Mark III model and the preparation of this study involved extensive research assistance from Susanna Mursula and Dirk Muir, who provided outstanding support. Norma Alvarado and Helen Hwang also played major roles in the project, preparing the manuscript and shepherding it carefully toward publication. Elisa Diehl of the External Relations Department edited the study and coordinated its production. The authors alone are responsible for the shortcomings of the model and its analysis; the opinions expressed are theirs and do not necessarily reflect the views of the IMF.

I Introduction

Overview

MULTIMOD (MULTI-region econometric MODel) was initially designed to analyze the macroeconomic effects of industrial country policies on the world economy. Since it was first described and documented by Masson and others (1988), the model has been extended in a number of directions, primarily for the purpose of increasing its usefulness in assisting with the IMF's multilateral surveillance over the policies of its members. A first set of revisions and extensions of the model, leading to MULTIMOD Mark II, was described by Masson, Symansky, and Meredith (1990). A number of additional changes have subsequently been implemented and were recently consolidated into MULTIMOD Mark III.

This paper describes the Mark III generation of MULTIMOD and its key properties in a manner intended to be intelligible to a wide spectrum of macroeconomists. It includes a discussion of the evolution, philosophy, and basic structure of the model (Section II), sections on the major innovations in the core version of MULTIMOD Mark III (Sections III–VII), and a discussion of several extensions of the model and the applications for which they have been developed (Section VIII). A summary description is provided in Box 1. Other boxes present selected simulations describing the responses of macroeconomic variables to different types of shocks; see table of contents. The results of additional "standard simulations" that can be performed on the model (and compared with Mark II simulations)—as well as a technical guide to MULTIMOD that will be of interest primarily to economists engaged in constructing and simulating structural macroeconometric models—will be provided on the IMF's internal Web site and will be released at some point on its external Web site (http://www.imf.org). The Web sites will also be used as vehicles for disseminating information in a timely manner about future extensions of MULTIMOD. It is anticipated that MULTIMOD will continue to evolve over time, not only as a reflection of ongoing efforts to refine the behavioral equations of the model, but also to incorporate changes in the core set of countries and country groups.[1]

What's New?

Macroeconometric models evolve for at least four reasons. The first simply reflects the fact that the initial stages of model construction necessarily involve simplifications, and the passage of time provides opportunities for specification improvements and extensions of coverage. A second reason is that the leading issues for macroeconomic policy evolve with the performance of economies and the thinking of economists, challenging the model builder to anticipate and adapt. A third reason is that access to new or more extensive data sets facilitates the empirical evaluation of behavioral hypotheses. And fourth, advances in computer hardware and software, and in algorithms for solving large nonlinear systems of equations, continue to loosen the technical constraints on the scale and complexity of the models.

The Mark III version of MULTIMOD differs from its predecessor in several important respects. New features include a core steady-state analogue model, a new model of the inflation-unemployment nexus, an extended non-Ricardian specification of consumption-saving behavior, and improved specifications and estimates of investment behavior and international trade equations. In addition to these changes in model specification, the introduction of a new solution algorithm has greatly increased the robustness, speed of convergence, and accuracy of the simulations and made it easier to develop certain modified versions of MULTIMOD that were difficult to solve with the Mark II algorithm.

Because the theoretical foundations of MULTIMOD include the premise that economic agents

---

[1]Work on a more extensive disaggregation of the developing and transition economies is under way, and changes in the core set of industrial countries and country groups will be required in the context of European Economic and Monetary Union.

Box I. MULTIMOD: Summary of the Mark III Generation

MULTIMOD is a dynamic multicountry macro model of the world economy that has been designed to study the transmission of shocks across countries as well as the short-run and medium-run consequences of alternative monetary and fiscal policies. It has several variants, the current versions of which are referred to as the Mark III generation. The core Mark III model includes explicit country submodels for each of the 7 largest industrial countries and an aggregate grouping of 14 smaller industrial countries. The remaining economies of the world are then aggregated into two separate blocks of developing and transition economies. Extended versions of MULTIMOD include separate submodels for many of the smaller industrial countries, and work has been initiated on expanding the analysis of the developing and transition economies.

The basic structure and properties of MULTIMOD are meant to represent well-established views about how modern industrial economies function and interact with each other. A consistent theoretical structure is employed for all industrial economies, and cross-country differences in the behavior of agents (or the functioning of markets) are reflected in different estimated parameter values. The model converges to a balanced-growth path that is characterized by a full stock-flow equilibrium in which debtor countries service the interest payments on their net foreign liabilities with positive trade balances.

The MULTIMOD modeling system includes a well-defined steady-state analogue model for each country and for the world economy as a whole. These steady-state models serve two roles. First, they are used to construct terminal conditions for the dynamic models. Second, they can be used to study the long-run effects of shocks that have permanent consequences for saving, capital formation, output, real interest rates, real exchange rates, and so on. The basic structure of MULTIMOD is simple enough that it is fairly straightforward to estimate additional country models for the smaller industrial economies.

Despite the focus on medium- and long-run properties, MULTIMOD also exhibits important short-run Keynesian dynamics that result from significant inertia in the inflation process. The MARK III generation features a nonlinear relationship between unemployment and inflation that reflects short-run capacity constraints and insider-outsider influences on wage setting. The asymmetric property of the Phillips curve provides a fundamental role for stabilization policies that is absent from linear models of the business cycle.

MULTIMOD assumes that behavior is completely forward looking in asset markets and partially forward looking in goods markets, but it is possible to study the effects of shocks under alternative assumptions about expectations formation and the degree of policy credibility. The model is solved with state-of-the-art simulation algorithms that have been designed specifically for such systems of equations.

Consumption-saving behavior is based on an extended Blanchard-Weil-Buiter paradigm in which

---

form their expectations in a forward-looking manner, the medium- and long-run properties of the model have an important influence on its predictions of the short-run responses to exogenous policy adjustments or other shocks. In this connection, one of the important new features of the Mark III generation is its more appealing approach to defining the long-run properties of the model's baseline path. As noted in Section II, the database for MULTIMOD simulations consists of the projections over a five-year horizon from the IMF's *World Economic Outlook*. In constructing a baseline path for MULTIMOD Mark II, the projected behavior of economic variables beyond that horizon was constrained to be consistent with the simplifying assumptions that primary fiscal and trade balances converge gradually to zero (thereby gradually stabilizing the stocks of public and international debt relative to GDP) and that the real rate of interest converges to the steady-state rate of growth.

These assumptions are not imposed in constructing baselines for MULTIMOD Mark III. Instead, as described in Section III, the projected behavior of

economic variables beyond the five-year horizon of the *World Economic Outlook* is tied to terminal conditions determined endogenously and consistently from a system of steady-state analogue equations, SSMOD. Among other things, SSMOD has the property that the real interest rate exceeds the rate of growth,[2] and so MULTIMOD is now capable of providing a more appealing characterization of the macroeconomic effects of fiscal adjustments and a richer analysis of sustainability issues.

MULTIMOD Mark II did not focus explicitly on the unemployment rate and characterized inflation simply in terms of the GDP deflator, with no atten-

---

[2]A no-Ponzi-game condition—that asymptotically the real interest rate must exceed the growth rate—is often imposed in optimizing models that are used for policy analysis; see, for example, the discussions of basic infinite-horizon models and overlapping-generations models in Blanchard and Fischer (1989). In MULTIMOD, the difference between the steady-state levels of the real interest rate and the growth rate depends on the parameters of the production function, the rate of depreciation, the rate of time preference, and the level of world government debt.

agents are assumed to have finite planning horizons. The model has been extended to allow for realistic age-earnings profiles and for the fact that a significant proportion of consumption is constrained by disposable income insofar as households are unable to borrow against future labor income streams.

Investment behavior is based on Tobin's q theory, according to which the desired rate of investment exceeds the steady-state rate as long as the expected marginal product of capital is greater than its replacement cost. The model allows for significant adjustment costs.

MULTIMOD has a standard specification of import and export behavior that embodies the notion that countries trade in diversified products. Import volumes are a function of the main components of aggregate demand, with import contents of the different components calibrated on the basis of information from input-output tables. Exports are modeled to approximately represent the mirror image of the foreign import demand functions.

Exchange rates and interest rates are related by an adjusted interest parity condition that can allow for persistent risk premiums. MULTIMOD provides a fundamental role for the real exchange rate, both in equilibrating aggregate demand and supply in the goods market and in ensuring that flow relationships are consistent with consumers' desired rates of asset accumulation. The short-run properties of the model to some extent mimic the properties of the Dornbusch overshooting model insofar as asset market prices are free to jump, while wages and other prices are characterized by stickier intrinsic and expectational dynamics.

The fiscal policy instruments include government absorption, distortionary capital taxes, and nondistortionary labor taxes (labor supply is exogenous). In the core version of MULTIMOD, government absorption is exogenous and the aggregate tax rate is endogenized to ensure that the ratio of government debt to GDP converges to a target level. However, in the short run, it is possible to treat all three fiscal instruments as exogenous variables.

Given the forward-looking nature of MULTIMOD, the fundamental role of the monetary authorities is to provide an anchor for inflation expectations. This can be accomplished in many ways. Options available in the core version of Mark III include fixed exchange rates, money targeting, inflation targeting, and nominal income targeting.

MULTIMOD has not been designed to be a forecasting tool. The baseline corresponds to the medium-term *World Economic Outlook* projections, which reflect the detailed knowledge and judgments of the IMF's country economists. These medium-term projections are then extended into a model-consistent balanced-growth path where the real interest rate is greater than the world real growth rate.

MULTIMOD is available to the public and can be obtained through e-mail to multimod@imf.org.

tion to the consumer price index (CPI). This has now changed, giving MULTIMOD several other new features. In particular, as described in Section IV, Mark III includes a new model of the inflation process. The domestic GDP deflator is determined by an expectations-augmented Phillips curve, and the CPI is determined by a weighted combination of the prices of domestically produced goods and the prices of imported goods. The Phillips curve relationship is asymmetric around the natural rate of unemployment, which has important implications for the design of macroeconomic stabilization policies.

Thanks to a debate rekindled by Barro (1974), it has become widely appreciated over the past two decades that the effects of fiscal policy on macroeconomic behavior in a forward-looking model depend on the extent to which the private sector expects that public sector imbalances will be evened out over time, so that an increase in the current fiscal deficit, for example, can be anticipated to imply a higher future tax burden, other things equal. However, the sensitivity of private sector behavior to policy adjustments can also depend importantly on factors other than the nature of expectations. In this regard, a second new feature of MULTIMOD Mark III is the manner in which the specification of consumption-saving behavior reflects the composition of wealth, the finite life cycles of households, and constraints on the ability of households to borrow against their future lifetime income streams. In Mark II, private consumption was assumed to be directly proportional to the sum of human wealth (that is, discounted after-tax labor income) and financial wealth, with human wealth discounted over an infinite horizon. In Mark III, the hypothesized behavior of private consumption has been modified in several respects, as described in Section V, embodying the assumptions that individual households optimize their consumption-saving behavior over finite lifetimes and face liquidity constraints on their abilities to borrow against future income. The two key parameters of the new consumption-saving model—the intertemporal elasticity of substitution and the share of consumption that is sensitive to disposable income—are estimated from the time-series properties of consumption after a realistic structure is imposed on life-cycle age-earnings profiles obtained from cross-sectional data.

The macroeconomic effects of policy actions or other exogenous shocks depend importantly on the responsiveness of aggregate demand to interest rates and exchange rates. Accordingly, finding realistic specifications for the behavior of investment and international trade volumes and, in particular, capturing their sensitivities to interest rates and exchange rates are key challenges in macroeconomic modeling. In this regard, MULTIMOD Mark III reflects efforts to improve the specifications of both the investment and the trade equations, as described in Sections VI and VII.

II The Philosophy and Basic Structure of MULTIMOD

What does fiscal consolidation imply for domestic output growth and inflation, and what are the spillover effects on other economies? To what extent do the macroeconomic consequences depend on whether fiscal consolidation is achieved through expenditure reductions or tax increases? How do the reactions of monetary authorities influence the outcomes? How sensitive are the effects of fiscal consolidation to the magnitude of the associated changes that take place in market interest premiums, which reflect, inter alia, the "market's" degree of confidence about the prospects for macroeconomic stability? How should monetary authorities react, in the absence of constraints on their discretion, to an unexpected decline in the saving rate or to the loss of productive capacity associated with a natural disaster? How do different forms of monetary policy "rules" compare in terms of their implications for the expected levels and variances of output growth and inflation rates? These are some of the issues that central banks and other policy authorities confront in their attempts to promote price stability and macroeconomic growth.

Over the past several decades, a number of policymaking institutions and academic researchers have developed macroeconometric models to help shed light on such issues.[3] These models provide frameworks that can take account of many aspects of macroeconomic behavior simultaneously, allowing model builders to explore the implications of their preferred theories of economic behavior while also imposing macroeconomic consistency on the analysis.

Philosophical Underpinnings

Considerable variety has emerged in the underlying philosophies and basic structures of the macroeconometric models that different modeling groups have chosen to develop. Among other things, this variety has reflected differences in three related considerations: the importance attached to short-term forecasting among the possible purposes that the models have been constructed to serve; the assumptions that have been adopted in the treatment of expectational variables; and the attitudes that model builders have taken toward the Lucas critique (see Lucas, 1976)—that is, toward the possibility that the coefficients in econometric equations may be altered by changes in policy regimes.

MULTIMOD has been designed to assist the IMF with its multilateral surveillance over the macroeconomic policies of member countries, but not to provide short-term forecasts. As such, its main purpose is to analyze how the effects of policy actions are transmitted over the medium term with particular interest in the analysis of actions by countries where policy adjustments have relatively large spillover effects on the world economy.

Unlike models that are designed to generate their own forecasts of a set of endogenous variables based on historical data and assumptions about the future evolution of various exogenous variables, MULTIMOD incorporates an externally generated baseline forecast of the world economy that reflects the detailed knowledge and judgments of the IMF's country economists. The baseline forecast is updated on a regular basis in association with the process of preparing the IMF's semiannual *World Economic Outlook* reports.[4] Once the baseline forecast is specified, MULTIMOD can be used to ana-

---

[3]Among the earliest of these models, each focusing on only a single economy, were Klein and Goldberger (1955), Klein and others (1961), and Duesenberry and others (1965). Bryant, Hooper, and Mann (1993) provides descriptions of, and references to, a number of the multicountry macroeconometric models that are currently in use; see also Edison, Marquez, and Tryon (1987), Gagnon (1991), Helliwell and others (1990), McKibbin and Sachs (1991), and Meredith (1989).

[4]The procedure for making a system of estimated equations consistent with an externally generated baseline forecast essentially involves solving for, and imposing, a set of residuals under which the estimated model generates the baseline solution. Strictly speaking, the *World Economic Outlook* baseline projects only over a five-year horizon. The manner in which the baseline path is extended beyond this horizon is discussed in Section III.

lyze the effects on that baseline of scenarios that involve changes in policies in major countries or certain other exogenous changes in the macroeconomic environment.

Because MULTIMOD is designed to analyze how a prespecified baseline forecast would be affected by policy changes or other exogenous shocks, the model can abstract from many of the special factors that are often present in forecasting models, and that likewise need to be taken into consideration in generating the *World Economic Outlook* projections that provide the judgmental baseline for MULTIMOD.[5] The ability to abstract from many special factors subsumed in the baseline forecast endows MULTIMOD with the virtue of simplicity, which is an attractive characteristic. Simplicity makes it easier to comprehend and assess the results of model simulations and also reduces the computer capacity and time required to solve the model.

Models that are relied upon to generate short-term forecasts are sometimes constrained to adopt compromises in specification forms—including in their treatment of expectational variables—for purposes of improving their accuracy as short-term forecasting tools. MULTIMOD has not been so constrained; its component equations have been estimated in forms that can be regarded, for the most part, as structural equations derived from models of optimizing behavior.[6]

The treatment of expectations in macroeconometric models has been an area of considerable controversy. The main alternative to assuming that expectations are forward looking and model consistent is to base the specification of expectations on backward-looking regressions of relevant variables on historical values of themselves and other variables. Most models, including MULTIMOD Mark III, incorporate a mixture of the two extremes,[7] but typically with a strong inclination toward one extreme or the other. Advocates of adaptive backward-looking expectations, who tend to place high priority on short-term forecasting accuracy, have argued that macroeconometric models with model-consistent

expectations perform relatively poorly in replicating the observed persistence and variability in business cycles. This argument is not very forceful, however, for models like MULTIMOD, in which inflation expectations reflect a mixture of backward-looking and model-consistent (forward-looking) elements, since such models are capable of generating large and persistent business cycles. Advocates of model-consistent expectations argue that their models are less vulnerable to the Lucas critique than models with backward-looking expectations. The validity of this criticism, however, is also difficult to judge. Those who reject it point out that the Lucas critique is simply "a possibility theorem, not an existence theorem," claiming that an "extensive search of the literature reveals virtually no evidence demonstrating the empirical applicability of the Lucas critique" (Ericsson and Irons, 1995, p. 39).

We are not comforted by the latter argument. It is easy to derive nonsensical policy implications from mechanical simulations of any model that embodies a reduced-form specification of inflation expectations, particularly when the latter specification does not include a forward-looking model-consistent component. For example, models that embody a Phillips curve and the assumption that inflation expectations are entirely backward looking, which is convenient and fairly common in the macroeconometric models used by central banks and other national authorities,[8] can lead mechanically to policy inferences that are inconsistent with the implications of the long-run natural rate hypothesis (LR-NRH). Indeed, a number of economists have argued that faulty logic, associated with the use of macroeconomic models that embodied backward-looking inflation expectations and thereby failed to provide a channel for "regime changes" to affect inflation expectations realistically, was largely responsible for excessive monetary accommodations in the 1970s.[9]

---

[5]Indeed, in many contexts the effects of shocks, measured as deviations from the baseline path, are largely independent of the specific baseline forecast.

[6]Loosely speaking, the main criteria for incorporating an estimated equation specification are that the specification should be based to a large extent on underlying theory and should not generate an unrealistic degree of macroeconomic variability when embedded into the MULTIMOD system of equations. Thus, in comparison with models for which short-term forecasting accuracy is a high priority, MULTIMOD has been estimated with a relatively low willingness to sacrifice theoretical foundations in order to obtain better goodness of fit.

[7]See Helliwell (1993). Model-consistent expectations appear to be relatively more attractive for asset markets, and adaptive expectations more popular for markets with greater inertia in price adjustment.

[8]For example, the Federal Reserve Board's FRB/Global Model (see Levin, Rogers, and Tryon, 1997) relies on backward-looking ("limited-information") expectations as its base case, although it can also be simulated under the assumption of model-consistent expectations.

[9]Among those who blame misleading economic theories for the "great inflation" in the United States in the late 1960s and 1970s, Taylor (1996, p. 184) notes that during that period, "the idea that there is a long-run Phillips curve trade-off began to appear in textbooks, newspapers, and even the *Economic Report of the President*; the inflation cost of an overheated economy, according to this theory, was simply a higher rate of inflation, not rising inflation." Studies by economic historians, such as De Long (1996), add support for this view by rejecting the alternative hypothesis that supply shocks (especially oil price shocks) were the main source of the rise in inflation. Taylor also emphasizes the coincidence in timing between the monetary disinflation of the 1980s and the incorporation into macroeconomics of more reasonable models of expectations and price adjustment, attributable largely to research started by Lucas (1972).

MULTIMOD has fixed weights on backward- and forward-looking components for inflation expectations, which reflects an attempt to separate intrinsic dynamics (in particular, the inertial effects of wage-price contracting lags) from expectational dynamics.[10] This specification can also lead mechanically to nonsensical policy inferences, which makes it incumbent upon model users to reflect on the appropriateness of the fixed-weight specification for the type of analysis that is being undertaken and perhaps to vary the weights (to capture credibility effects) in certain policy experiments. For example, under a mechanical application of MULTIMOD that treated announced inflation targets as completely credible (that is, that set inflation expectations equal to the announced inflation targets), a Ponzi-game policy of announcing future disinflation but repeatedly postponing the implementation could generate the nonsense result of a free lunch—a drop in inflation with no loss of output or an opportunity to lower interest rates and achieve both inflation reduction and output gains. Although the scope for such nonsense could be reduced by replacing the fixed-weight specification of inflation expectations with a model in which expectations reflected the credibility of monetary policy, appropriately defined, at present macroeconomists do not have a firm understanding of how such a model should be specified.

The treatment of inflation expectations, with a positive weight on model-consistent forward-looking expectations, makes MULTIMOD consistent with the LR-NRH. This gives MULTIMOD the property of money neutrality: money supply or price level shocks have no effect on the steady-state values of real variables, other things equal. To a close approximation, MULTIMOD also exhibits monetary superneutrality: as long as inflation rates remain moderate, changes in the rate of growth of the money supply have almost no effect on the steady-state values of real variables.[11]

While MULTIMOD's formulation of inflation expectations attempts to capture the inertial effects of wage-price contracting lags, as well as forward-looking elements, the core version of Mark III uses pure forward-looking model-consistent solutions for exchange rate and interest rate expectations in the interest parity equation and the term structure equations. The assumption that asset-market expectations are completely model consistent is unrealistically strong, although at this stage we regard it as more attractive than the available alternatives.[12] However, Mark III has been coded in a manner that allows users to modify the treatment of expectations; it is straightforward to model exchange rate and interest rate expectations as blends of backward- and forward-looking components and to allow for time-varying weights in modeling inflation expectations.

The long-run properties of models with forward-looking expectations have been difficult to study in the absence of steady-state analogue models. With the arrival of Mark III, such a steady-state analogue model has now been developed for MULTIMOD,[13] as described in Section III. The steady-state model can be used both as an interpretive device for understanding long-run comparative statics and to determine model-consistent terminal conditions for dynamic analysis.

Simulations of Mark III—which involve simultaneous solutions of both the steady-state model and the dynamic model—can be regarded as follows. The solution to the steady-state model represents a position of simultaneous stock and flow equilibrium. Loosely speaking, households determine the steady-state level of wealth, firms determine the stocks of physical capital, governments determine the levels of their debts, and, for each country (or block of countries), the reconciliation of these stock positions comes through the net foreign asset position. In this context, the reconciliation of stocks and flows in the long-run steady state, both within countries and for the world as a whole, imposes conditions on the steady-state levels of real exchange rates and interest rates. Real exchange rates must be consistent with generating the trade and current account flows that are associated with steady-state stocks of net foreign assets (or ratios of net foreign assets to GDP), while the level of interest rates must be consistent with global balance between saving and investment or, equivalently, with global consistency between net foreign asset stocks and current account flows.

The solution of the dynamic model describes the evolution of macroeconomic variables en route to full stock and flow equilibrium. Given the long-run equilibrium values of the endogenous variables in

---

[10]By intrinsic macroeconomic dynamics, we mean those dynamics that may be assumed to be invariant to the types of policy experiments that are being considered. Of course, for enormous changes in policy rules, contract length as well as the degree of nominal indexation may change, and it then becomes difficult to determine precisely what is structure. However, by assuming that inflation expectations partly reflect the model-consistent solution, MULTIMOD at least makes some attempt to control for the first-order effects of the Lucas critique.

[11]The departure from strict superneutrality reflects the fact that MULTIMOD embodies an "inflation tax."

[12]In this regard, analysis of how rational agents form expectations when it takes time to learn about the nature of various policy changes and other exogenous shocks remains an important area for additional research.

[13]In this respect, the methodology for solving MULTIMOD Mark III is similar to that for solving the Bank of Canada's Quarterly Projection Model—see Laxton and Tetlow (1992) and other references cited in Section III.

MULTIMOD, as determined from the steady-state analogue model, the time paths of the endogenous variables are determined by solving the dynamic model under the assumption of model-consistent forward-looking expectations.[14] The solution process involves an iterative procedure that imposes consistency between the model's final solution values for the endogenous variables and its simultaneous solutions for the values of ex ante expectations about these variables.

History and Country Disaggregation

The development of MULTIMOD was a continuation of work on a precursor model known as MINIMOD (see Haas and Masson, 1986). The precursor model was disaggregated into two regional blocks—the United States and an aggregate rest-of-the-industrial-world region—with the equations for each region based on the same theoretical framework. The parameters of MINIMOD were obtained not by direct estimation but rather by simulation of a more extensive model with a quarterly database.

Unlike MINIMOD, MULTIMOD is largely estimated and uses annual data. The first published version of MULTIMOD (see Masson and others, 1988) divided the world into seven blocs: the United States, Japan, Germany, an aggregate of the other Group of Seven industrial countries, an aggregate of the remaining industrial countries, a group of high-income oil-exporting developing countries, and an aggregate of the remaining developing countries. This country disaggregation reflected both the priorities that were attached to modeling the effects of policy changes in the largest countries, which tend to have the greatest spillover effects on the world economy, and the relatively limited availability of data for developing countries. For the same two reasons, the models for the developing country blocs were specified with relatively little detail on monetary and fiscal policy variables, but with emphasis on trying to capture realistically the behavior of the current account positions of these blocs in order to be able to impose a realistic consistency constraint on world saving and investment.

The country disaggregation in MULTIMOD has been extended over time. Both the Mark II and the core Mark III versions include separate models for each of the Group of Seven countries, an aggregate of the remaining industrial countries, and the two groups of developing countries. As an alternative to treating the industrial countries other than the Group of Seven

as a single bloc, a modified version of the Mark II model, which includes 14 individual European countries, has been developed for analyzing issues relating to the European Union.[15] By contrast, only limited analysis has been conducted with the two developing country blocs. Apart from redefining the bloc of high-income oil exporters,[16] the aggregation scheme for the developing and transition economies remains the same as in the Mark I version.[17]

Commodity Disaggregation and Behavioral Units

MULTIMOD can be regarded as a slight modification of a model in which each industrial country (or bloc of industrial countries) produces a single differentiated product—its "main composite good," which is perceived to be an imperfect substitute for other countries' main composite goods. The industrial country models disaggregate oil from total production and absorption, but oil production for these countries is treated as exogenous and most macroeconomic variables of interest are not significantly affected by the behavior of oil consumption. The main developing country model, as well as the international trade accounts, distinguishes among three categories of tradable goods—main composite goods, oil, and primary commodities other than oil—and, in addition, the main developing country block includes nontradables as a fourth category of goods.[18] The inclusion of explicit behavioral hypotheses about production (or net exports) of oil, primary commodities, and nontradables in the main developing country model, along with an explicit hypothesis about the availability of external finance to the main group of developing countries, adds important elements of reality to MULTIMOD's characterization of the aggregate current account position of the developing countries and, thus, the equal and

---

[14]As noted earlier and elaborated in Section V, inflation expectations are only partially forward looking.

[15]See Masson and Symansky (1992), Masson and Turtelboom (1997), and the discussion in Section VIII below.

[16]In Mark III, the group comprises six high-income oil exporters—Kuwait, Libya, Oman, Qatar, Saudi Arabia, and United Arab Emirates—corresponding to the *World Economic Outlook* group of capital-exporting developing countries. The work program for the near future includes redefining the aggregation scheme for the nonindustrial economies and enhancing the models of their macroeconomic behavior.

[17]A modified version of the Mark II model disaggregates the main developing country bloc into four separate groups: Western Hemisphere, Africa, the group of four newly industrialized economies, and an aggregate of the other non-oil developing countries. See Bayoumi, Hewitt, and Symansky (1995) and the discussion in Section VIII below.

[18]The group of net creditor developing countries is assumed to produce only oil.

opposite aggregate current account position of the industrial countries.

Each of the industrial country models is structured around five types of behavioral units: households, firms, nonresidents, the fiscal authorities, and the monetary authorities. Households supply labor, consume domestically produced and imported goods, and accumulate wealth. Firms hire labor, invest, and produce output for domestic and foreign markets. Nonresidents engage in international trade and financial borrowing and lending with domestic residents. The fiscal authorities control the level of government spending, choose a target trajectory for government debt, and set tax rates consistent with government spending and the debt target. The monetary authorities guide short-term nominal interest rates according to postulated reaction functions that may be specified in a variety of ways.

The Supply Side and the Unemployment-Inflation Nexus

Many of the macroeconometric models that are currently employed in policymaking institutions include well-articulated supply sides along with Phillips curve relationships that hypothesize a short-run trade-off between inflation and unemployment while also embodying the restrictions of the long-run natural rate hypothesis (that is, the hypothesis of no long-run trade-off). Most of these cases, however, incorporate *linear* short-run Phillips curves, which are difficult to reconcile with observed asymmetries in labor market data, and which also substantially weaken the rationale for short-run stabilization policies. By contrast, the core Mark III version of MULTIMOD includes *nonlinear* Phillips curves.

As in Mark II, the Mark III production function for each country's main composite good is specified as a Cobb-Douglas relationship between capacity output and two factor inputs—the labor force and the real net capital stock—with a constant growth rate of total factor productivity. The labor supply is exogenous, and the solution for the unemployment rate reflects, inter alia, the short-run Phillips curve and equations that describe the dynamic evolution of inflation expectations and the nonaccelerating inflation rate of unemployment (NAIRU); see Section IV for further discussion.

Consumption, Investment, and International Trade

The demand side of the industrial country models is largely described in Sections V–VII, which focus respectively on the behavior of consumption, invest-

ment, and international trade in countries' main composite goods. The supplies of, and demands for, oil and primary products in industrial countries, and the structure of the developing country models, are described later in this section.

The aggregate consumption function for the main composite goods (Section V) is based on an optimizing model of life-cycle behavior. The main variables explaining a country's consumption are its human wealth (the expected discounted value of current and future after-tax labor incomes plus any transfers from the government) and its nonhuman wealth (physical capital plus claims on the government plus net foreign assets).[19] Individual consumers are assumed to have model-consistent expectations about their future after-tax income streams, but also to have finite lives. The latter property implies that fiscal policy actions have non-Ricardian effects on the economy. The model incorporates a nonlinear relationship between labor earnings and age (estimated from data for the United States), in which an individual's relative earnings rise in the early part of his working life and subsequently decline. In the core version of Mark III, it is assumed that households face liquidity constraints on their abilities to borrow against their future incomes, which augments the non-Ricardian properties of the model.[20]

Investment demand (Section VI) is modeled in the spirit of Tobin (1969), extended by allowing for adjustment costs, with the net change in the capital stock reflecting the gap between the market value of existing capital and its replacement cost. Gross investment equals net investment plus depreciation, where the rate of depreciation is exogenous.

The volume of imports of main composite goods (Section VII) depends on both relative prices and a measure of domestic activity. The activity variables used in the Mark III trade volume equations (unlike the normal unweighted measures used in many trade equations, including the Mark II specifications) are weighted sums of the components of ag-

---

[19]The discount rate that enters the calculations of human and nonhuman wealth includes the exogenous rate of population growth and the after-tax interest rate applicable to saving (the nominal riskless rate of interest plus a premium that reflects both the credit risk on personal income and the probability of death).

[20]As discussed in Section V, the issue of whether fiscal policy has non-Ricardian effects continues to be actively debated as an empirical proposition. The rationale for adopting the Mark III consumption-saving specification in a model used for policy analysis comes partly from the appeal of the theoretical framework, but also reflects a balancing of the prospective welfare costs of type 1 and type 2 policy errors. Fiscal policy actions based on erroneous prescriptions from a non-Ricardian model when the "true model" was Ricardian would presumably tend to be less costly than fiscal policy inaction based on erroneous analysis with a Ricardian model when the "true model" was non-Ricardian.

gregate domestic absorption (that is, private consumption, private fixed investment, and government expenditure) and exports, where the weights reflect import propensities calculated from recent input-output matrices for each country. In reality, for many countries, the data show large differences among the import shares of the different expenditure components, and for these cases this new feature of the trade volume equations can significantly enhance the plausibility of MULTIMOD's analysis of the macroeconomic effects of changes in government expenditure. In addition to their dependence on domestic absorption, import volumes are related to the ratio of the import price deflator to the deflator for non-oil GNP.

For purposes of consistency, MULTIMOD specifies each country's export volume equation in a form that broadly resembles the import volume equations of its trading partners. In particular, export volumes are related to two variables. The first is a foreign activity variable, defined as a weighted average of foreign-country import volumes (where the weights reflect the base-period shares of the home country's exports accounted for by the foreign countries or country groups). The second variable is a real competitiveness index, defined as a weighted sum of the logarithms of export prices of a country's trading partners relative to home-country export prices (where the weights capture the sensitivity of home-country exports to competition in third markets from foreign countries). The latter price measure is based on the IMF's Information Notice System trade weights.[21]

Fiscal Policy: Government Spending, Taxes, and Debt

For each industrial country, the basic fiscal policy instruments in MULTIMOD are generally specified as the level of real government spending, a basic tax rate defined as the ratio of total tax revenues to nominal GDP, and the tax rate on capital income.[22] The effective tax rate on labor income can be derived from the basic tax rate and the tax rate on capital income; a number of other fiscal variables—including the budget balance and the stock of government debt—are constructed from the spending and tax rate variables through various definitional identities.[23] When simulating the effects of fiscal policy changes, the fiscal variables need to be adjusted in a consistent manner. This is illustrated in Box 2, which examines the spillover effects of a 10 percent increase in government debt that is generated by temporarily reducing taxes by 2 percent of GDP for five years.

The settings of the fiscal policy instruments are not based on estimated behavioral equations. In most simulations, however, the behavior of the basic tax rate is governed by a reaction function (or feedback rule) with imposed parameters. The inclusion of such a reaction function is intended to preclude unrealistic model solutions in which the stock of government debt grows without bound relative to GNP.[24] The specification in the core Mark III model (which is unchanged from the Mark II specification) assumes that the basic tax rate is adjusted in response to both the level of, and the change in, the gap between the actual ratio of government debt to GNP and an exogenous target ratio of government debt to GNP.[25] The parameters of the reaction function, which were originally chosen on the basis of earlier work that studied the dynamics of MINIMOD (see Masson, 1987), are set at levels that make the model stable and, in particular, that tend to induce the ratio of government debt to GNP to return to its baseline path over the horizon typically used for model simulations. By changing the specification and parameters of this feedback rule, MULTIMOD can be applied to study and compare the stabilizing properties of different types of fiscal policy reaction functions.

Monetary Policy

MULTIMOD can be simulated under a variety of monetary policy reaction functions. The Mark III model treats short-term nominal interest rates as monetary policy instruments and can accommodate interest rate adjustment rules that are consistent with either fixed exchange rate bands, money targets, inflation targets, nominal income targets, or other macroeconomic objectives, including combinations of inflation and output or employment objectives.

For many applications, it has been traditional to include two different forms of monetary policy reaction functions in simulations of MULTIMOD Mark II.

---

[21]Measures of nominal and real effective exchange rates are also constructed in MULTIMOD using the IMF's Information Notice System weights (for a description of these weights, see McGuirk (1987) and Zanello and Desruelle (1997)).

[22]For the developing country blocs, the public and private sectors are essentially treated as an aggregate, with no separation between government spending and private spending and no explicit treatment of taxes.

[23]One of the modified versions of MULTIMOD (see Section VIII) includes indirect taxes as well as the direct taxes on labor and capital incomes.

[24]For some purposes, it is appropriate to "turn off" the tax rate reaction function and to allow debt to accumulate under a constant basic tax rate.

[25]See the discussion in Masson, Symansky, and Meredith (1990), pp. 11–12.

For France, Italy, and the aggregate of industrial countries that are not part of the Group of Seven, the monetary authorities have been assumed to adjust short-term interest rates in response to movements in their exchange rates vis-à-vis the deutsche mark. For the United States, Japan, Germany, the United Kingdom, and Canada, the monetary authorities have been assumed to adjust short-term interest rates in response both to the gap between a target for the stock of money and its actual value and to the gap between potential output and actual output.

Although money targeting is no longer widely practiced among industrial country central banks, the traditional reaction function specifications remain the "default option" for the core Mark III model and are the basis for most of the illustrative simulations presented in this paper.[26] These traditional specifications can easily be modified by model users. The reason that they remain in the core model is that we have not yet been able to undertake the detailed country-by-country analysis that seems warranted before replacing the present default options with a new set of specification forms and parameter values.[27]

It is widely recognized that, in reality, the macroeconomic effects of unexpected shocks can depend importantly on how policymakers react. Consistently, the effects of shocks in MULTIMOD depend intimately on the assumptions about monetary policy reaction functions, so that any "quantification" of multipliers in MULTIMOD is conditional on the nature of the monetary policy response. Box 3 illustrates the degree to which key government expenditure multipliers in the Mark III model are sensitive to the nature of monetary policy reaction functions.

Partly in light of such sensitivity and because we intend to change the reaction functions in the core model over the next year or so, we provide only a limited set of simulation results in this paper. However, interested readers can find a more extensive set of "standard simulations" at the MULTIMOD Web sites, and can compare these Mark III simulations with analogous Mark II simulations reported in Appendix I of Masson, Symansky, and Meredith (1990).[28]

---

[26]As with the fiscal policy feedback rules, the parameters of these monetary policy reaction functions are imposed, with parameter values set at levels that make the model stable.

[27]We plan to undertake such an analysis over the next year in conjunction with regrouping some of the industrial countries in the context of European Economic and Monetary Union.

[28]To the extent that the Mark III and Mark II models embody the same reaction functions, comparisons of "standard simulations" of the two models can be revealing. However, for models with forward-looking expectations, which take account inter alia of the nature of policy behavior, the optimal forms of monetary policy reaction functions are model specific, and one can question the meaningfulness of comparing standard simulations of models with either different optimal policy reaction functions or common suboptimal reaction functions.

Money supplies in MULTIMOD are described by a single monetary aggregate for each industrial country—the monetary base—which includes both currency and the reserves of commercial banks held with the central bank.[29] The estimated money demand equations relate (the logarithm of) real money balances—the monetary base divided by the absorption price deflator—to (the logarithm of) real domestic absorption and the short-term nominal interest rate. The money demand equations for the industrial countries were estimated jointly (see Masson, Symansky, and Meredith, 1990, pp. 12–13). These equations affect the macroeconomic responses to shocks only in cases in which monetary policy reaction functions are assumed to involve interest rate adjustments in response to deviations of money supplies from target paths.

Oil, Primary Commodities, and Nontradables

MULTIMOD recognizes that the performance of the world economy can be affected considerably by changes in the prices of oil or non-oil primary commodities and also that net exports (or imports) of these goods can be important components of the external balances of individual countries and country groups. In contrast to its treatment of main composite goods, for which each country is assumed to produce a differentiated composite, MULTIMOD assumes that oil and non-oil primary commodities are each homogeneous goods with a single world market price. The price of oil is treated as exogenous, while the price of primary commodities is perfectly flexible and varies endogenously to clear the market.

The global supply of oil is assumed to be perfectly elastic at the world market price. Oil production by each of the industrial countries, however, is treated as exogenous (perfectly inelastic), whereas production by the two developing country blocs is assumed to respond passively to the global demand for oil at the given price, with the net exports of each of the two blocs providing a fixed proportion of the excess of industrial country demand over industrial country supply.[30]

---

[29]Neither of the developing country models contains a monetary sector.

[30]These assumptions, which are retained from the Mark I model, are consistent with the paradigm that the Organization of Petroleum Exporting Countries sets the price of oil and serves as residual supplier. It may be noted that inventories of oil are not explicit in the model; changes in inventories are implicitly included in consumption.

Box 2. The Spillover Effects of Government Debt

Increasing international financial integration has expanded the markets in which governments can sell their debt. In principle, this development provides greater scope for governments to smooth taxation and spending and for countries to smooth consumption over time in the face of temporary shocks. But capital market integration also implies that the fiscal policies of one country will affect other countries. In a world with highly integrated capital markets, a country that issues an amount of debt that is globally significant will thereby raise real interest rates throughout the world and crowd out private investment in all countries. An important policy implication is that countries that issue large stocks of debt not only may reduce their own living standards, but also may impose significant spillovers on other countries by pushing up the world real interest rate.

Recent empirical evidence has found significant effects of world government debt on real interest rates. (See, for example, Tanzi and Fanizza, 1995; and Ford and Laxton, 1995.) This is consistent with other empirical evidence suggesting that government deficits reduce national and world saving because consumers increase their saving by less than the full amount of the future taxes that will be necessary to finance the higher level of debt. As a consequence, there will be a tendency to overconsume available resources, with resulting higher real interest rates and a lower world capital stock. This tendency to overconsume available resources in the short run by reducing the capital stock also lowers the sustainable level of consumption in the long run.

Box 9 provides a more extensive discussion of the aggregate crowding-out effects of the buildup in government debt in the industrial countries, along with estimates suggesting that there could be very significant benefits for the world economy if governments reduced their debts. Here, we focus on the spillover effects of one country's debt on living standards in other countries.

To illustrate, the table presents estimates of the own-country effects and spillover effects that would be asso-ciated with a temporary five-year tax cut that increases the debt-to-GDP ratio of the United States by 10 percentage points.[1] Specifically, taxes are reduced by 2 percent of GDP for five years, and then allowed to rise to stabilize the debt-to-GDP ratio at a steady-state level that is 10 percentage points higher than the baseline level.[2] The simulations are based on monetary policy reaction functions that broadly resemble the policy environment of the early 1980s, with monetary targets in Canada, Germany, Japan, the United Kingdom, and the United States and fixed exchange rates (versus the deutsche mark) in France and Italy.

As seen in the table, in the short run, lower taxes result in strong expansion of real consumption and GDP in the United States, with positive spillover effects on the world economy. With higher real interest rates, however, capital accumulation slows in both the United States and other industrial countries, and by year 4 real GDP levels are below baseline, with steady-state GDP 0.3 percent below baseline in the United States and 0.4 percent below baseline in other industrial countries. Steady-state consumption is 0.7 percent below baseline in the United States and 0.2 percent below baseline in other industrial countries, reflecting the effects of lower per capita real income. The long-run effects on consumption are larger in the United States because net foreign assets fall in the United States and rise in the other countries.

---

[1]To put the size of this shock into perspective, the ratio of net debt to GDP of the United States increased from an average of 26 percent during 1978–80 to 56 percent in 1995; see International Monetary Fund (1996).

[2]This is implemented through adjustment of the basic tax rate on nominal GDP, holding constant the tax rate on capital income. In the steady state, the basic tax rate must exceed the baseline level to finance the increased interest burden that results from higher government debt and higher interest rates.

The specification of oil consumption by industrial countries is based on estimates, using pooled data, of an error-correction model in which the same long-run and short-run price elasticities and long-run activity elasticities are imposed across all countries. The short-run responses of oil consumption to activity, as measured by GDP, are allowed to differ across countries. The long-run elasticity with respect to GDP is constrained to be unity, while the long-run elasticity with respect to the relative price of oil (that is, the ratio of the price of oil to the country's GDP deflator) is estimated to be less than unity (in absolute value). The specifications and estimated coefficients are described in more detail in Masson, Symansky, and Meredith (1990, pp. 6–7).

MULTIMOD includes the production of non-oil primary commodities, which represents only a small share of the aggregate output of the main developing country group (but is relatively important for some regions within this group). Output (and exports) of primary commodities by the main developing country bloc reflects productive capacity, which is treated as perfectly inelastic in the short term but responsive over time to changes in relative price (or, implicitly, to changes in the profitability of production).[31] The industrial countries and the high-income oil export-

---

[31]The paradigm is a crop harvest or production from mines, where individual producers are too small to influence the price and where the marginal costs of expanding contemporaneous supply are infinite.

Effects of a Five-Year Temporary Tax Cut That Permanently Increases the Debt-to-GDP Ratio of the United States by 10 Percentage Points

	Year 1	Year 2	Year 3	Year 4	Year 5	Steady State
Real GDP						
United States	0.7	0.3	—	−0.1	−0.1	−0.3
Other industrial countries	0.3	0.1	−0.1	−0.1	−0.1	−0.4
Capital stock						
United States	—	−0.2	−0.4	−0.6	−0.8	−1.2
Other industrial countries	—	−0.1	−0.2	−0.3	−0.3	−1.2
Real interest rate (10-year)						
United States	0.6	0.6	0.6	0.5	0.4	0.1
Other industrial countries	0.2	0.2	0.2	0.2	0.2	0.1
Consumption						
United States	1.3	1.1	0.9	0.9	1.0	−0.7
Other industrial countries	0.4	0.2	—	−0.1	−0.2	−0.2
Unemployment rate						
United States	−0.3	−0.2	−0.1	—	—	—
Other industrial countries	−0.1	−0.1	—	—	—	—
GNP deflator						
United States	0.3	0.7	1.2	1.6	1.8	0.8
Other industrial countries	−2.3	−2.1	−1.8	−1.4	−0.7	1.6
Net foreign assets						
United States	0.1	—	−0.2	−0.4	−0.7	−5.6
Other industrial countries	0.4	0.4	0.5	0.6	0.7	2.9
Real exchange rate						
United States	2.2	2.2	2.1	1.8	1.2	−0.9
Other industrial countries	−1.0	−1.0	−0.9	−0.8	−0.5	0.5

Note: In percent deviations from baseline for all variables except the real interest rate and unemployment rate, which are percentage point deviations from baseline.

ing countries are treated as if they do not produce primary commodities.[32] The industrial country consumption (and import) equations for primary commodities are based on an error-correction model that regresses the change in imports on (current and lagged) changes in GDP and relative prices, as described in more detail in Masson, Symansky, and Meredith (1990, pp. 7–8). The price of primary commodities is perfectly flexible and clears the market.

For the main developing country bloc, MULTIMOD also identifies a composite nontradable good.

Insofar as these countries are assumed to face a balance of payments financing constraint (described below), the presence of a nontradables sector is important for capturing the expansionary effects of export growth. The demand for nontraded goods in the main developing country bloc reflects an assumption that consumption and investment are split (in endogenously determined proportions) between nontradables and other goods. Output of nontradables is assumed to be perfectly elastic (entirely demand determined) at an exogenous price; there is no capacity constraint on nontradables production, and there is assumed to be sufficient slack in the developing country economies to increase the output of nontradables without shifting resources out of other sectors. Without such scope to expand the production and

[32]Implicitly, any actual outputs and exports of primary commodities by the industrial countries are aggregated with their outputs and exports of the main composite goods.

Box 3. Government Expenditure Multipliers Under Alternative Monetary Policy Reaction Functions

This box illustrates the effects of an increase in government expenditure under alternative assumptions about monetary policy. The simulations are conducted on the Japan bloc of the model. The specific experiment that we consider is a permanent increase in government expenditures of 1 percent of baseline GDP[1] that results in a 10 percentage point increase in the ratio of government debt to GDP. For the first 10 years of the shock, tax rates are held fixed; in the eleventh year, the basic tax rate is allowed to rise to stabilize the debt-to-GDP ratio. The main point of the box is that there is no such thing as a pure fiscal shock; the short-term effects of fiscal policy depend intimately on the reaction of the monetary authorities. To illustrate, we consider three possible assumptions for monetary policy: exchange rate targeting, inflation targeting, and money targeting. In each case, we assume that the authorities rely on a short-term interest rate as the instrument to adjust in pursuing their target.

Money targeting and exchange rate targeting can be implemented in Mark III by specifying the following reaction function,

$$rs_t = rs_{t-1} + \alpha(m_t - m_t^*) + \beta(er_t - er_t^*),$$

where rs is the short-term nominal interest rate, m is the level of money balances (in logs), er is the nominal exchange rate, and the asterisks denote the desired levels of money balances and the nominal exchange rate. A fixed exchange rate can be imposed by choosing a very large value for β and setting α equal to zero. Similarly, it is possible to keep money balances close to their desired levels by setting β equal to zero and choosing an appropriate value for α. For the case of money targeting, we have chosen a value for α that keeps money balances close to desired levels but does allow small deviations from the targets in the short run.

For present purposes, we define inflation targeting broadly as a rule that adjusts the short-term nominal interest rate in response to changes in expected inflation and movements in both the inflation rate (π_t), and the output gap (y_t), where inflation is measured using the GDP deflator. This is implemented with the following equation,

$$rs_t = rr_t^* + \pi_t^e + \mu(\pi_t - \pi_t^*) + \nu(y_t - y_t^*)$$

where rr_t^*, π_t^*, and y_t^* are the baseline values for the real interest rate, the inflation rate, and the output gap, and π_t^e is the level of inflation expectations. For illustrative purposes, we focus on the case $\mu = \nu = 1$.[2]

The table reports the shock-minus-control values for real GDP, money balances, the short-term interest rate, the nominal exchange rate, and the GDP deflator. Under each of the three reaction functions, the shock has positive short-run effects on real GDP and the GDP deflator, although the magnitudes of these effects depend on the particular reaction function. Under fixed exchange rates, real GDP increases by more than the increase in government expenditures in the first year. In this case, because the monetary authorities are targeting the nominal exchange rate, short-term interest rates are unchanged and the increase in nominal aggregate demand implies a significant increase in the level of nominal money balances.

The short-run effects on GDP are considerably smaller under money targeting and inflation targeting, because monetary conditions tighten to counteract the expansionary effects of the shock. Under money targeting, short-term interest rates increase by 40 basis points in the first year and this, combined with a 4.0 percent appreciation of the yen, reduces the short-run output effects from 1.5 percent to 0.6 percent. Under inflation targeting, the short-term interest rate increases by 100 basis points, the nominal exchange rate appreciating by

---

[1]Because of the nonlinear properties of Mark III, the effects of fiscal shocks depend on whether the economy is initially in excess demand or supply. These simulations were conducted on a baseline that assumes that output is equal to potential.

[2]These weights are fairly similar to the Taylor rule; see Taylor (1993).

---

consumption of nontradables, an expansion of developing country exports would not have significant multiplier effects on aggregate output, but would simply lead to an equal increase in imports.

Financing Constraints and Absorption for Developing Countries

As described earlier, MULTIMOD divides the developing and transition economies into a group of six high-income oil exporters and the main developing country bloc. The larger bloc, which includes a great majority of the IMF's developing country members, is assumed to face constraints on external financing.

The constraint on external financing, a legacy of the debt crisis of the 1980s, is a key feature of the main developing country model. The availability of financing is assumed to depend on the expected future growth of exports and on the gap between the prevailing ratio of net debt interest payments to exports and a long-run benchmark level of that ratio.[33] In combination, the availability of external

---

[33]Debt interest payments are calculated net of interest receipts on international reserve assets.

Effects of a 1 Percent of GDP Permanent Increase in Government Expenditure in Japan Under Alternative Monetary Policy Reaction Functions

	Year 1	Year 2	Year 3	Year 4	Year 5
Real GDP					
Exchange rate target	1.5	1.2	0.4	−0.2	−0.5
Inflation target	0.4	—	−0.1	−0.2	−0.2
Money target	0.6	0.1	−0.1	−0.2	−0.3
Money supply					
Exchange rate target	1.3	3.1	4.4	5.0	4.9
Inflation target	−0.4	−0.3	−0.1	0.2	0.4
Money target	—	0.3	0.4	0.5	0.5
Short-term nominal interest rate					
Exchange rate target	—	—	—	—	—
Inflation target	1.0	0.7	0.6	0.5	0.5
Money target	0.4	0.4	0.4	0.4	0.3
Nominal exchange rate					
Exchange rate target	—	—	—	—	—
Inflation target	4.8	3.9	3.2	2.6	2.0
Money target	4.0	3.7	3.3	2.9	2.5
GDP deflator					
Exchange rate target	1.1	2.7	4.0	4.7	4.8
Inflation target	0.2	0.6	0.9	1.2	1.5
Money target	0.3	0.7	1.0	1.1	1.2

Note: In percent deviations from baseline for all variables except the short-term interest rate, which is percentage point deviations from baseline.

4.8 percent, and there is an even smaller increase in output in the first year.

Under fixed exchange rates, the nominal exchange rate is not free to jump in response to the changing cyclical conditions of the economy, and, with forward-looking exchange rate expectations and interest rate parity, there is no pressure for the nominal interest rate to change; the adjustment process thus takes consider-

ably longer. In this case, movements in real monetary conditions can be affected only by movements in the price level, and because prices are sticky in MULTI-MOD, fiscal expansions can result in a significant and persistent business cycle. By contrast, under inflation targeting, the short-run effects of the shock are considerably smaller and the economy returns to potential considerably faster.

financing, the level of exports, and the level of net debt interest payments impose a constraint on the sum of imports and the change in international reserve holdings. A second relationship between the latter two variables, in which the ratio of international reserves to imports adjusts over time toward a target level, is included in the core version of MULTIMOD to determine the balance between imports and the change in reserves.

Absorption in the main developing country model is disaggregated only into consumption and investment; private and government demands are not distinguished in the data, and there is no role for fiscal or monetary policies. Consumption is assumed to

depend on a measure of current and lagged disposable income that includes the available flow of external financing. The latter incorporates changes in the net foreign asset position and debt levels, including valuation effects arising from changes in interest rates and exchange rates. Investment is determined from the national income accounts residually as the sum of domestic saving (production minus consumption) and net saving from abroad (imports minus exports). Implicitly, however, the determination of the supply of external financing (net saving from abroad) in a forward-looking framework takes into account the marginal product of capital in contributing to the expected future growth of exports.

Consumption and investment expenditures by the main group of developing countries are assumed to reflect demands for both main composite goods and nontradable goods. Investment purchases are allocated between increments to capital in the main composite goods sector and capital accumulation in the non-oil primary commodities sector; nontraded goods and oil are assumed to be produced without capital goods. The allocation of investment among sectors depends on the relative price of main composites and primary commodities, which is regarded as an indicator of the relative rates of return in the two sectors.[34] Once in place, capital is assumed to be immobile between sectors.

For the bloc of six high-income oil-exporting countries, it is assumed that imports are not constrained by available external financing. Their outputs of main composites and non-oil primary commodities are not treated explicitly, and the price of their domestic output is identified with the price of oil.

Consistent with the lack of explicit treatment of non-oil output, the model for the high-income oil exporters includes specific equations for imports of main composites and non-oil primary commodities, but does not explicitly model the domestic demands for main composites or primary commodities. Import volumes are assumed to depend, however, on aggregate domestic activity variables, as well as on the ratio of the price of imports to the price of oil.

Accounting Identities, Arbitrage Conditions, Interest Rates, and Exchange Rates

As consistency requirements, MULTIMOD imposes both the national income accounting identities that individual country models must satisfy and a parallel set of identities at the global level. At the national level, the difference between saving and investment must equal the current account balance or,

equivalently, the sum of net exports of goods and nonfactor services plus net receipts from factor services and transfers. At the global level, saving and investment must be equal, such that national current account balances sum to zero.

MULTIMOD also imposes two types of arbitrage conditions on interest rates and exchange rates. One of these constrains each country's long-term nominal interest rate to be consistent with the time path of its expected short-term interest rates. The core version of MULTIMOD requires that the long-term interest rate equal the expected return from holding a series of comparable short-term securities, but it is possible to introduce modifications that allow for liquidity or risk premiums. The second type of arbitrage condition links interest rates and exchange rates. The core model imposes the uncovered interest parity condition, requiring that interest rate differentials (on equal-maturity assets denominated in two different currencies) equal expected rates of change in exchange rates (between the same two currencies), but this can be modified to allow for interest premiums.

The accounting identities play a major role in determining the steady-state values of interest rates and exchange rates. Loosely speaking, one can think of the identity between global saving and global investment as a condition that pins down the steady-state values of real interest rates—that is, nominal interest rates adjusted for expected changes in price levels (absorption deflators). Similarly, one can think of the identities between national saving-investment balances and current account positions as conditions that pin down the steady-state values of real exchange rates. And, given the expected long-run equilibrium (that is, steady-state) values of interest rates and exchange rates, together with the assumption that expectations about interest rates and exchange rates are model consistent, one can think of the two sets of arbitrage conditions as pinning down the entire expected future time paths of interest rates and exchange rates.[35]

---

[34]Neither the data nor the model is adequate for considering other factors relevant to the sectoral allocation of investment.

[35]This description is oversimplified, of course, because it takes as given the steady-state levels of saving and investment. In general, the steady-state values of saving, investment, and most other variables depend on exogenously specified assumptions about certain variables and key parameters; see Section III.

III The Steady-State Analogue Model and Mark III Solution Methodology

As noted in Section I, the Mark III version of the model incorporates a major advance in the treatment of the long-run properties of MULTI-MOD. Unlike in previous generations, each of the dynamic equations in MULTIMOD Mark III has a steady-state analogue equation. The system of steady-state analogue equations, SSMOD, is maintained separately from the system of dynamic equations, DYNMOD.[36]

The addition of SSMOD strengthens the properties and analytic capabilities of MULTIMOD in several important ways. SSMOD can be used both as an interpretive device for understanding long-run comparative statics and as a vehicle for determining model-consistent terminal conditions for dynamic analysis. Moreover, in any model that embodies forward-looking expectations, such as MULTIMOD, the medium-run responses of macroeconomic variables to exogenous policy changes or other shocks are influenced by the long-run properties of the model; thus, the quality of the dynamic analysis generated by a forward-looking model depends importantly on whether the long-run properties of the model have solid theoretical foundations and on whether the dynamic equations and their steady-state counterparts are specified consistently. Both of these features have been achieved in MULTIMOD Mark III.

To illustrate these points, the next subsection describes two dynamic equations in MULTIMOD and derives the steady-state analogue equations. The remainder of the section then discusses the use of SSMOD as an interpretive device for understanding long-run comparative statics and medium-term dynamics, the manner in which SSMOD is used to generate a control path that extends the baseline scenario from the *World Economic Outlook* and converges to a model-consistent steady state, the advantages of using a steady-state model to obtain terminal conditions, and the Mark III solution methodology.

An Example of Parallel Equations in DYNMOD and SSMOD

Consider the following two dynamic equations:

$$\frac{CA_t}{Y_t} = \frac{TB_t}{Y_t} + r_t \frac{NFA_{t-1}}{Y_t} \tag{1}$$

and

$$\frac{CA_t}{Y_t} = \frac{NFA_t - NFA_{t-1}}{Y_t}. \tag{2}$$

Equation (1) is a balance of payments identity that expresses the current account balance (*CA*) as the sum of the trade balance (*TB*) and the interest receipts on net foreign assets (*NFA*), where *r* denotes the nominal interest rate, the subscripts denote time periods, and all three terms in the equation have been scaled by the level of nominal GDP (*Y*). For illustrative purposes, we assume that interest receipts are paid on a short-term financial asset that rolls over each period, with the nominal interest rate in period t applied to the outstanding net claims on foreigners that exist at the end of period $t - 1$.[37] Dividing both sides of the balance of payments identity by *Y* allows us to provide some illustrative calculations for the usual case in which nominal GDP is expanding over time. Equation (2) is just an identity that equates the current account balance to the change in net foreign assets.

To derive the analogue equations for SSMOD, let g denote the steady-state growth rate of all nominal variables, such that $NFA_{t-1} = NFA_t /(1 + g)$. Substitut-

---

[36]In moving to a modeling system with parallel dynamic and steady-state equations, Mark III has followed in the footsteps of other national and two-region models that have been designed for policy analysis. For examples of such models and some relevant applications, see Laxton and Tetlow (1992), Black and others (1994), Bryant (1996), Coletti and others (1996), Faruqee, Laxton, and Symansky (1997), Bryant and Zhang (1996a, 1996b), and Black and others (1997).

[37]This simplification is made for expositional purposes. In Mark III, the rate of return on net foreign assets is a blend of the rate of return on a short-term debt instrument and the rate of return on a long-term debt instrument.

Box 4. Government Debt, Net Foreign Liabilities, and the Real Exchange Rate

In the core version of Mark III, real interest rate *differentials* in the long run are assumed to be independent of the stocks of government debt.[1] Thus, government debt in a particular country will influence real interest rates in the long run only if it affects global saving and investment and the *level* of the world real interest rate. For small countries, such global effects will likely be small, but they may be significant for larger countries; Box 2 illustrates the spillover effects of an increase in government debt in the United States. Moreover, while the worldwide effects of the government debt of an individual country may be small, a debt buildup in several industrial countries could have important combined effects on global saving, global investment, and the world real interest rate, as illustrated in Box 9.

The table presents estimates of the long-run effects of changes in the ratio of government debt to GDP for each of the major industrial countries.[2] In each of the two panels, the debt-to-GDP ratio is increased by 10 percentage points for individual countries, one at a time. These increases are achieved through temporary tax cuts; in the long run, tax rates must rise to finance the higher interest burdens that result from higher levels of government debt.[3] The top panel provides estimates derived from the individual country models in isolation, abstracting from any induced effects on, or feedback from, the rest of the world, and thus assuming that the equilibrium world real interest rate is fixed. In the second case, the results are derived from the full multicountry model, with the steady-state world real interest rate adjusting endogenously to equate world saving and investment.

As shown in the top panel, with the world real interest rate fixed, an increase in government debt (in percentage points of GDP) translates into roughly the same increase in net foreign liabilities in the steady state. The increase in debt initially induces a rise in the domestic interest rate and an appreciation of domestic currency, which affects the current account and leads to the buildup of net foreign liabilities over time. To service the resulting higher interest payments to foreigners in the steady state, there must be a larger net flow of goods and nonfactor services from the home country to foreigners (recall equation (5)). And under normal assumptions about intertemporal consumption preferences, this implies that the real exchange rate must depreciate in the long run, more so for relatively closed economies (in particular, Japan and the United States) than for other cases.

For the unconstrained simulations summarized in the lower panel, the endogenous world real interest rate rises by up to 11 basis points, with the extent of the increase depending primarily on the size of the country in which the debt increase occurs. In this case, the expan-

---

[1]Endogenous country-specific risk premiums are not included in the core version of Mark III because empirical estimates of their behavior were too unappealing. However, users of Mark III can easily incorporate their own assumptions about risk premiums, and the model can be used to compare the macroeconomic implications of alternative assumptions. For examples, see Laxton and Tetlow (1992); Bayoumi and Laxton (1994); Black and others (1994); Macklem, Rose, and Tetlow (1995); and Laxton and Prasad (1997).

[2]The dynamic effects of government debt in a small open economy are discussed in Box 9.

---

[3]For each country, the basic tax rate on aggregate nominal GDP is reduced by 2 percentage points for five years and is then allowed to rise, while the tax rate on capital income is held constant at its baseline level.

---

ing this latter condition into equations (1) and (2) provides the steady-state analogue equations.

$$\frac{CA}{Y} = \frac{TB}{Y} + \frac{r}{(1+g)}\frac{NFA}{Y} \qquad (3)$$

and

$$\frac{CA}{Y} = \frac{NFA}{Y}[g/(1+g)]. \qquad (4)$$

The Steady-State Model as an Interpretive Device

The steady-state model can provide an important interpretive device for understanding long-term comparative statics and medium-term dynamics.

Consider, for example, an application of equation (4). If all nominal variables in the economy are growing at 5 percent in the steady state and net foreign assets are equal to 100 percent of GDP, the current account surplus must be a little less than 5 percent of GDP. Conversely, a net debtor country would be running a current account deficit in long-run equilibrium. If we combine equations (3) and (4) we can obtain an equation that links a country's steady-state trade balance to its level of net foreign assets.

$$\frac{TB}{Y} = \left(\frac{g-r}{1+g}\right)\frac{NFA}{Y}. \qquad (5)$$

The interpretation of this equation is straightforward. In long-run equilibrium, under the steady-state condition that $r > g$ (see discussion below), when the ratio of a country's net foreign assets (or li-

Long-Run Effects of Temporary Tax Cuts That Permanently Increase Debt-to-GDP Ratios by 10 Percentage Points

	Net Foreign Liabilities[1,2]	Current Account Balance[1,3]	Trade Balance[1,3]	Real Competitiveness Index[2]	Real Interest Rate[4]
Single-country model results					
Canada	10.0	−0.5	0.2	−0.2	—
France	10.8	−0.5	0.3	−0.5	—
Germany	10.9	−0.5	0.3	−0.5	—
Italy	10.1	−0.5	0.2	−0.4	—
Japan	11.5	−0.5	0.3	−1.9	—
United Kingdom	9.9	−0.5	0.2	−0.3	—
United States	10.1	−0.5	0.2	−0.7	—
Full multicountry model results					
Canada	9.9	−0.5	0.2	−0.2	1
France	10.4	−0.5	0.3	−0.5	2
Germany	10.2	−0.5	0.2	−0.4	3
Italy	9.7	−0.5	0.2	−0.4	2
Japan	9.1	−0.4	0.2	−1.2	7
United Kingdom	9.3	−0.4	0.2	−0.3	2
United States	5.6	−0.3	0.2	−0.7	11

[1]As a percent of nominal GDP.
[2]Percent deviation from baseline.
[3]Percentage point deviation from baseline.
[4]Basis point deviation from baseline.

sionary effect of the tax cut partly spills over on the rest of the world, putting upward pressure on foreign interest rates and dampening the initial exchange rate appreciation. Accordingly, the shock has a smaller effect on the current account, and the steady-state level of net foreign liabilities increases less than in the first set of simulations, especially for larger countries such as the United States.

abilities) to GDP is stable, the country will receive (or pay) net income on its international asset (or liability) position that is a constant fraction of its GDP. The payments received by a net creditor country will finance a steady-state trade deficit, with imports exceeding exports. Conversely, payments by a net debtor country to its creditors will require a steady-state trade surplus.

These implications of equation (5) provide important intuition for understanding the sensitivity of the long-run equilibrium level of the real exchange rate to shocks that affect the desired net foreign asset position of the economy. This is illustrated in Box 4, which describes the long-run effects of changes in the ratios of government debt to GDP; the speeds with which different types of variables converge to steady-state values following a shock are illustrated

later. In a fully specified intertemporal model that attains a full stock-flow equilibrium, the steady-state levels of the trade balance and the real exchange rate will reflect the desired net foreign asset position of the economy. Thus, an increase in desired net foreign liabilities caused by an increase in government debt will require a larger trade surplus in order to finance the higher interest obligations. And this can be obtained only if the real exchange rate depreciates in the long run.

On Using SSMOD to Construct the Control Solution

In previous generations of MULTIMOD, behavior beyond the *World Economic Outlook* projection hori-

---

Box 5. Traditional Solution Techniques and the MARK III Methodology

The numerical complexity of solving a small-scale rational expectations model is equivalent to that of solving very large scale backward-looking econometric models. To make such a task manageable, traditional algorithms were designed to break large blocks of simultaneous equations into smaller pieces and then to use an iterative procedure to ensure consistency across blocks until the full system converged.

The traditional Fair-Taylor (1983) algorithm separated the problem into three types of iterations, and a Gauss-Seidel iterative procedure was relied upon to solve each layer of iteration. The problems with this approach are well known; it can be time consuming and is not guaranteed to find a solution even when a well-defined saddle-point stable solution exists; see Armstrong and others (1998). Indeed, practitioners using this technique have frequently been forced to rely heavily on certain tuning parameters (ordering, convergence tolerance limits, damping factors, divergence factors, and so on) to help the algorithms achieve convergence in a reasonable amount of time. At the same time, these difficulties have made it unattractive to rely on certain classes of models for which the problems are particularly severe. In practice, this has meant that model builders until recently have had to either linearize their models or restrict their attention to issues that could be dealt with more easily with traditional algorithms. However, the enormous advance in computer technology over the last few years has made it possible to design and implement more robust methods for solving medium-sized nonlinear models that feature model-consistent expectations; see Armstrong and others (1998) and Juillard and others (1998).

The development of the Mark II version of MULTIMOD was done principally with an extended Fair-Taylor (F-T) algorithm. This algorithm used the Newton-Raphson method to solve for Type I iterations and a Gauss-Seidel iterative scheme to solve for the simultaneity that arises from model-consistent expectations. Juillard and others (1998) show that with the Newton-Raphson-based Laffargue-Boucekkine-Juillard (L-B-J) algorithm, fairly accurate solutions for Mark II can be obtained in two iterations, and that in most cases the model converges in about four or five iterations with extremely accurate solution values. This should not be surprising, however, because the Mark II version did not contain many significant nonlinearities; in such cases, one should expect that a Newton-Raphson-based algorithm would obtain extremely accurate solutions in a few iterations.

The L-B-J approach involves stacking the equations—or combining the Type I and Type II iterations in the F-T algorithm—and then employing a method first proposed by Laffargue (1990), then developed by Boucekkine (1995), Juillard (1996), and Hollinger (1996), to exploit information about the repetitive and sparse structure of the full simultaneous problem. The results in Juillard and others (1998) will be very encouraging to anyone who is interested in building medium-sized macro models designed for policy analysis. They report significant savings of time in comparison with traditional and extended F-T algorithms, even when fairly loose conventional convergence tolerance limits are allowed for F-T. Second, they show that when the F-T convergence tolerance is tightened sufficiently to approximately replicate the L-B-J solutions, the relative time savings of the L-B-J algorithm become enormous.

These results understate the potential benefits of a state-of-the-art algorithm like the L-B-J algorithm because the tests were performed on the Mark II version of MULTIMOD, which was developed with an extended F-T algorithm. The Mark II version is approximately linear in that it generally only takes a few L-B-J iterations to achieve full convergence for a large set of shocks. Juillard and others (1998) discuss a few cases where MULTIMOD development has been impeded because F-T had difficulty finding solutions. Here, the relative comparison becomes more difficult because it depends on how adept the user is at tuning certain parameters to achieve convergence, and this depends on the particular shock and model under consideration.

The solution methodology for Mark III is based on the following two steps. First, terminal conditions are

---

zon was constrained to be consistent with the imposed assumptions that the primary fiscal and trade balances converge gradually to zero (thus eventually stabilizing the stocks of public and net international debt relative to GDP) and that the real rate of interest converges to the steady-state rate of growth. The latter condition, while extremely convenient for creating a baseline control solution, had the undesirable feature of making fiscal policy a Ponzi game. In particular, governments could issue long-term debt with no apparent real costs, because such debt could always be rolled over at real interest rates that were no greater than the steady-state growth rate.[38]

---

[38]If the real interest rate was less than the growth rate, there would be no real costs, and indeed there would be potential benefits, from delaying fiscal consolidation. In fact, if the real interest rate were less than the growth rate and independent of fiscal policy, a government could reduce tax rates, issue debt instruments, and allow growth in its tax base to eliminate the debt. For this reason, most theoretical optimizing models used for policy analysis impose a no-Ponzi-game condition; see, for reference, the discussion in Blanchard and Fischer (1989).

computed by solving the steady-state analogue models using a standard Newton-Raphson algorithm that exploits sparsity in the Jacobian. Second, the L-B-J algorithm is used to solve the dynamic model given initial conditions, shocks to the exogenous forcing processes, and estimates of the terminal conditions that are obtained from the steady-state models.

To illustrate the iterative process of the solution method, the figure shows the solution paths for the inflation rate and the unemployment gap (that is, the NAIRU minus the unemployment rate) following a 10 percent increase in the money supply in Germany when the world economy is initially in a position of full stock-flow equilibrium. Because long-run monetary neutrality holds in Mark III, a 10 percent increase in the money supply results in a 10 percent increase in the German price level, and all real variables eventually return to their baseline values.

In the short run, the effects of money supply shocks on the real economy can be quite significant and depend critically on the nature of the Phillips curve. In Mark III, the Phillips curve is convex and includes a binding short-run capacity constraint, so that extremely large expansionary money supply shocks have greater effects on the price level than they do on the unemployment rate. Conversely, negative money shocks have greater contractionary effects on the economy than positive money shocks of the same magnitude; Box 8 provides a discussion of the asymmetric effects of money shocks.

The figure reports the solution values for four iterations. The first iteration is obtained by linearizing the model around the control (or baseline) solution and then solving the linearized version of the model. The second iteration is obtained by linearizing the model around the solution values obtained from the first iteration; the iterative process continues until it converges. In the illustrated example, because the linearized short-run Phillips curve trade-off is flatter in the first iteration than it is in the neighborhood of the true solution, the decline in the unemployment rate in the first year is overestimated and the increase in the inflation rate is underestimated. The process

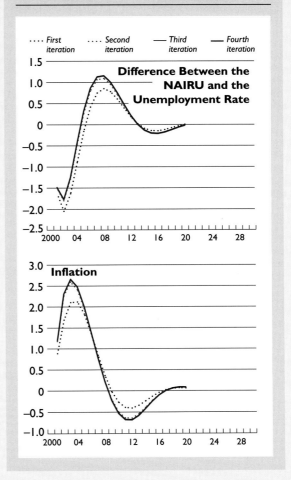

Convergence Properties of MARK III
(Deviations from baseline values, in percentage points)

···· First iteration ···· Second iteration —— Third iteration —— Fourth iteration

Difference Between the NAIRU and the Unemployment Rate

Inflation

continues in a very orderly manner and converges after a few L-B-J iterations.

In MULTIMOD Mark III, the extensions of the baseline control solution beyond the projection horizon of the *World Economic Outlook*, and the construction of model-consistent terminal conditions, also rely heavily on assumptions about the steady-state levels of the real interest rate and the rate of growth. These assumptions, however, can be modified. For the core version of Mark III, the baseline level of the steady-state real interest rate on short-term government debt (risk-free assets) is set at an imposed value of 4.25 percent—the average real rate of return that accrued during 1987–96 on the short-term public debts of the Group of Seven countries.[39] Furthermore, as in MULTIMOD Mark II, all countries are assumed to converge to a steady-state growth rate consistent with the *World Economic Outlook*'s projection of potential output growth for the United States.

---

[39]The real long-term interest rate in the steady state is assumed to be 5.25 percent, reflecting an assumption that the equilibrium term premium is 100 basis points.

Once the steady-state values of the real interest rate and the potential output growth rate are specified, SSMOD and DYNMOD are used to generate a complete baseline control solution (extending beyond the WEO horizon) with model-consistent terminal conditions. But the Mark III generation of MULTIMOD has the scope to explore the implications of alternative sets of terminal conditions—or, more precisely, of modifications in "exogenous assumptions" that lead to alternative sets of terminal conditions.[40] As was the case with the Mark II generation, MULTIMOD also has the scope to simulate and study the individual country SS and DYN models in isolation.[41]

On Using SSMOD to Obtain Terminal Conditions

In addition to strengthening the theoretical foundations of MULTIMOD and the consistency between its dynamic and steady-state behavior, the introduction of a steady-state analogue model has eliminated the scope for potentially large inaccuracies in solving for terminal conditions. The problem of poor terminal conditions has plagued forward-looking nonlinear models in general.

Box 5 discusses the difficulties of solving models with traditional techniques. In the past, users of MULTIMOD have had three choices for dealing with potential inaccuracies caused by poor terminal conditions. First, they could rely upon an iterative approach, such as Fair-Taylor Type III iterations, to eliminate the effects of inaccurate terminal conditions. Second, they could simply choose a simulation horizon that was sufficiently distant that any errors in the end point would have only a small impact on the solution values over the time period of interest.[42]

Third, users could guess new terminal conditions based on their understanding of the model. Each of the three approaches could be a time-consuming process, and there was no guarantee that the estimates were precise, especially if users were interested in obtaining estimates of the long-run comparative statics of the model. The introduction of SSMOD and new solution techniques has eliminated these problems.

The Mark III Solution Methodology

The development and use of forward-looking macro models in policymaking institutions have proceeded at a pace much slower than predicted in the early 1980s. An important reason is that researchers have not had access to robust and efficient solution techniques for solving nonlinear forward-looking models. The numerical complexity of solving a forward-looking macro model is considerably more onerous than solving a backward-looking model of the same size. Fortunately, the dramatic reduction in the cost of computer memory has made it possible to design better solution algorithms. Accordingly, MULTIMOD is now solved with a Newton-Raphson algorithm, which for nonlinear forward-looking models tends to converge much more rapidly and accurately than algorithms involving Gauss-Seidel iteration.[43] This technical advance has two related implications. By making Newton-Raphson iteration feasible, it avoids the large errors in convergence that sometimes arise under Gauss-Seidel iteration. In addition, with the introduction of an algorithm that is considerably faster and much less prone to simulation failures than its predecessor algorithms, it has become feasible for builders of nonlinear forward-looking models to increase the scope of their analytic frameworks. See Box 5 for additional discussion of MULTIMOD's new solution algorithm and its implications.

---

[40]This capability reflects advances in solution methodology.

[41]The TROLL programs used to create SSMOD and DYN-MOD for Mark III build up the world models by combining the codes of individual country models. This means that it is straightforward to simulate and study the individual country SS and DYN models in isolation. Obviously, this approach can save considerable time and computer resources in analyzing shocks where there are only second-order feedback effects across countries.

[42]The horizon over which variables converge to steady-state values in the baseline solution of the model may differ from the time it takes to achieve convergence in the shock-minus-control

---

values of the same variables. In the Mark III baseline, real interest rates and some real growth rates reach their steady-state values within 10 or 20 years, while demographics take more than half a century to settle down to a zero rate of population growth in all countries.

[43]See Juillard and Laxton (1996), and Juillard and others (1998) for a comparison of the properties of this algorithm with those of conventional first-order methods.

IV   The Inflation-Unemployment Nexus

A common criticism of the first generation of macroeconometric models is that they represented an incomplete macroeconomic paradigm because they failed to integrate a well-articulated "supply side" into the sticky-price Keynesian framework. In particular, because of the failure to impose adequate theoretical restrictions, most of these early models were dynamically unstable or did not have well-defined, long-run equilibrium properties; in some cases, for example, an increase in government spending could lead to implausible, never-ending expansions of output. Consequently, the first-generation econometric models have been discarded in policymaking institutions, and research has focused on investigating more thoroughly the channels through which policies affect macroeconomic aggregates in both the short term and the long term.

The second generation of macroeconomic models that were designed for policy analysis incorporated supply sides of varying complexity. A key element was generally a linear Phillips curve that hypothesized a short-run trade-off between inflation and unemployment while in many cases embodying the restrictions of the long-run natural rate hypothesis (LR-NRH)—that is, the hypothesis that the economy gravitates over the long term toward a natural rate of unemployment that cannot be reduced permanently by increasing either the level or the rate of growth of the money supply.[44]

The Short-Run Trade-Off Between Inflation and Unemployment

The hypothesis of a short-run trade-off between inflation and unemployment is consistent with considerable evidence that decisions to tighten monetary policy have been followed by reductions in both inflation and output growth (Romer and Romer,

1989). This raises the question of why monetary policy has effects on output in the short run. A plausible and popular answer is that nominal wages and prices are sticky in the short run, reflecting the existence of medium-term and perhaps overlapping wage contracts (Fischer, 1977; Taylor, 1980; Calvo, 1983). More fundamentally, price and wage stickiness may result from costs of changing individual prices or renegotiating wages (see the discussion in Fischer, 1994).

One way to specify a Phillips curve relationship is with the following two equations:

$$\pi_t = \pi_{t+1}^e + F(y_t) + \varepsilon_t^\pi \tag{6}$$

and

$$\pi_{t+1}^e = \Phi \, \pi_{t+1}^{mc} + [1 - \Phi]\pi_{t-1}, \tag{7}$$

where π_t is the rate of change of the non-oil GNP deflator during year t; π_{t+1}^e is the expectation during year t of inflation one year ahead; π_{t+1}^{mc} is the model-consistent solution for inflation one year ahead; y is the output gap; Φ is a nonnegative weight on the model-consistent solution; and ε^π is a stochastic error term. Equation (7) can be given several different interpretations. One interpretation is that $(1 - \Phi)$ represents the proportion of myopic agents who always use the previous year's inflation rate to forecast future inflation, while Φ represents the proportion of informed agents. Alternatively, equation (7) can be interpreted as a very simple learning model where Φ represents the speed at which agents learn the underlying structure of the economy and exogenous forcing processes. A third interpretation, perhaps more suitable to variants of equation (7) with additional lagged terms, views Φ as the proportion of medium-term overlapping wage contracts that are renegotiated in period t.

Many economists have argued that the Phillips curve is not a structural relationship, taking the view that no matter which of the above interpretations is adopted, Φ cannot be regarded as a "deep structural parameter" that is insensitive to the behavior of the monetary authorities. If monetary policy becomes highly inflationary, for example, the proportion of myopic agents would decline, the speed of learning

---

[44]Thus, the Phillips curve is vertical in the long run, and any attempt to hold unemployment below its natural rate will result in accelerating inflation; see Friedman (1968). The incorporation of a supply side into what was essentially a Keynesian paradigm is sometimes referred to as the "neoclassical synthesis."

would increase, and the prevalence and average duration of multiperiod nominal contracts would decline.

In practice, however, almost all macro models describe the supply side of the economy with a Phillips curve, given the strength of the empirical correlations in historical data and the lack of more attractive alternatives. This is also the case in MULTIMOD, which treats the Phillips curve as a structural relationship. That being said, we regard it as incumbent on model users to avoid subjecting their models to policy experiments for which the underlying assumptions about inflation expectations would break down.

When specifying a Phillips curve relationship in the form of equations (6) and (7), it is important to place a positive weight on the model-consistent expectation (that is, $\Phi > 0$). Otherwise, the model is inconsistent with the LR-NRH, since with $\Phi = 0$ it would always be possible for the monetary authorities to fool people systematically and raise the level of output in the long run by continuously increasing the rate of growth of the money supply.[45] The condition that $\Phi > 0$ implies that the long-run Phillips curve is vertical and that real variables, such as the unemployment rate, are tied down by real factors, such as tastes and technology, and are to a first approximation independent of both the level of the money supply (the condition of monetary neutrality) and the rate of growth of the money supply (monetary superneutrality). These long-run neutrality properties are an important trademark of MULTIMOD and several other prominent modern macroeconomic models.

Implications of Linear and Convex Phillips Curves

While the introduction of well-articulated supply sides has succeeded in pinning down the medium-term and long-term properties of macroeconometric models and clarifying the channels through which monetary and fiscal policies affect the economy in both the short run and long run, models with linear Phillips curves have been criticized on two important counts. First, they are inadequate by themselves for explaining certain prominent asymmetries in labor markets, such as the observation that unemployment rates appear to be stuck at high levels in a number of countries while examples of low unemployment equilibria seem rare. Second, they imply

that as long as policy authorities succeed on average in achieving a given target (or informal objective) for the rate of inflation, the speed and intensity with which stabilization policies react to unexpected shocks do not have first-order effects on the average levels of output and employment over time.

A number of industrial countries have experienced prolonged upward trends in unemployment that have persisted during much or all of the past three decades. Germany provides a good example. Although the unemployment rate has varied from year to year, each major economic downturn and subsequent recovery, or supply-side shock—such as the oil price hikes of the 1970s and German unification in the early 1990s—has ratcheted unemployment upward. While economists have long recognized that noncyclical unemployment can be the result of job search and market distortions—including regulations (for example, minimum wage rates and restrictive labor laws) and unionization—the observed phenomenon of upward trending unemployment rates has elicited attention over the past decade to theories that link the behavior of unemployment to factors that can plausibly generate a process of asymmetric hysteresis (Summers, 1988; Blanchard and Summers, 1986; Blanchard and Katz, 1997).

Such theories of the history-dependence of unemployment rates—and, in particular, of why an upward-trending proportion of the labor supply has not been absorbed or reabsorbed into the employed labor force—have focused predominantly on insider-outsider effects and human capital depreciation as likely explanatory factors. It has also been emphasized, however, that in the context of a nonlinear Phillips curve, the effectiveness of stabilization policies can interact importantly with other factors in explaining the upward trends in unemployment rates (Isard and Laxton, 1996; and Faruqee, Laxton, and Rose, 1998).

To provide an analytic framework in which stabilization policies can have first-order effects on the average levels of output and employment (at any given average inflation rate), the Mark III version of MULTIMOD continues to work within the confines of the long-run natural rate hypothesis, but features significant convexity in the short-run Phillips curve. This implies that the tradition of decomposing unemployment into structural and cyclical components requires modification, as does the traditional discussion of the nonaccelerating inflation rate of unemployment—the so-called NAIRU. To illustrate, Figure 1 shows a convex (to the origin) short-run Phillips curve, plotted as a relationship between expectations-augmented inflation (vertical axis) and the unemployment rate (horizontal axis), with expectations-augmented inflation corresponding to the difference

---

[45]In early versions of macroeconomic models, it was quite common to set Φ equal to zero because model builders did not have access to robust solution algorithms for solving models where agents were assumed to have some knowledge of the underlying structure and policy process.

Figure 1. A Convex Short-Run Phillips Curve

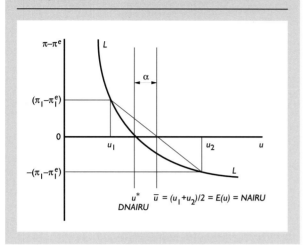

between actual and (ex ante) expected inflation.[46] The unemployment rate at which expectations-augmented inflation is zero—labeled u^* in Figure 1 and referred to as the DNAIRU or *deterministic NAIRU*—corresponds to the structural rate of unemployment that would prevail in a deterministic world. It is critical to recognize that the DNAIRU is not a feasible stable-inflation equilibrium in a *stochastic* economy with convexity. The average rate of unemployment that would be associated with nonaccelerating inflation (and expectations equilibrium) in a stochastic world—labeled $\bar{u}$ in the figure and referred to as the NAIRU—must lie above the DNAIRU. This is because convexity in the short-run Phillips curve means that inflation rises faster when unemployment is below the DNAIRU than it falls when unemployment is commensurately above the DNAIRU.[47] If u were maintained equal to u^* on average, the asymmetry in the response of inflation to symmetric aggregate demand shocks would make it impossible to maintain a constant average inflation rate.

The convex short-run Phillips curve combined with standard models of inflation expectations implies that stabilization policies that are successful in avoiding boom and bust cycles will reduce the average unemployment rate and raise the average level of output. This can be seen in Figure 1, which has been drawn

under the assumption that the unemployment rate is symmetrically distributed around the NAIRU over the range between u_1 and u_2. The important point is that success in reducing the variability of unemployment will also lower its mean value. One can see this immediately from Figure 1 by imagining a tighter control on the dispersion of unemployment. The line LL would move down and to the left and the gap between $\bar{u}$ and u^* would shrink. The key lesson is that stabilization can matter in the sense that policies that either induce or allow extreme variability in the business cycle will also cause a permanently higher NAIRU.[48]

With convex models of the Phillips curve, the analysis of unemployment behavior, in addition to identifying the cyclical variation of actual unemployment around its average rate, needs to recognize that the average rate of unemployment exceeds the structural rate of unemployment by an amount that generally reflects both the nature and the magnitude of economic shocks and the effectiveness of stabilization policies. With convexity in the short-run Phillips curve, stabilization policies can have permanent effects on unemployment and output.[49] When combined with more elaborate models of inflation expectations and imperfect policy credibility, the convex Phillips curve paradigm will hopefully provide a much richer macroeconomic framework for assessing the effectiveness of stabilization policies.[50]

Specification of the Mark III Phillips Curve

The Phillips curve in Mark III follows closely on the heels of some recent empirical work that has extended an estimation methodology proposed in Debelle and Laxton (1997) and applied to a fairly large group of industrial countries.[51] The empirical strat-

---

[46]The simple representation in Figure 1 abstracts from any lagged inflation terms.

[47]This type of convexity was an important feature of the original curve introduced by Phillips (1958) and discussed by Lipsey (1960) and several others. Macklem (1996) and Clark and Laxton (1997) provide a brief history of convexity in the Phillips curve and explain why it was overshadowed by other issues.

[48]If the degree of convexity in the short-run Phillips curve is independent of the long-term inflation objective, as in Mark III, then it will still be true that the long-run Phillips curve is vertical and the average unemployment rate will be independent of the target inflation rate. However, if convexity in the short-run Phillips curve becomes greater at very low inflation rates, as suggested by Akerlof, Dickens, and Perry (1996), then there may be a permanent trade-off between inflation and unemployment at low inflation rates.

[49]See Mankiw (1988) and De Long and Summers (1988).

[50]See Isard and Laxton (1996), and Callen and Laxton (1998).

[51]See also Isard and Laxton (1996), Clark and Laxton (1997), Debelle and Vickery (1997), Laxton, Rose, and Tambakis (1998), and Faruqee, Laxton, and Rose (1998). Studies by Laxton, Rose, and Tetlow (1993), Laxton, Meredith, and Rose (1995), Bean (1996), Turner (1995), Clark, Laxton, and Rose (1995, 1996), Macklem (1996), Fisher, Mahadeva, and Whitley (1996), Dupasquier and Ricketts (1997), and McDonald (1997) have also found evidence of asymmetries in the inflation process for several industrial countries using different empirical specifications.

egy is based on developing model-consistent measures of labor market tightness from the following convex functional form:

$$F(u_t^* - u_t) = \gamma \frac{(u_t^* - u_t)}{(u_t - \phi_t)}, \qquad (8)$$

where u is the unemployment rate, u^* is the DNAIRU, and γ and ϕ are parameters to be estimated.[52] Box 6 follows Faruqee, Laxton, and Rose (1998) in providing a derivation of the convex Phillips curve that is based on extending the model of Layard, Nickell, and Jackman (1991).

The Phillips curve represented by equation (8) has two asymptotes, at $u = \phi$ and $\pi - \pi^e = -\gamma$, as shown in Figure 1. The first represents the minimum level of unemployment where the short-run Phillips curve becomes vertical. The second asymptote, $-\gamma$, represents the point where marginal increases in unemployment have no additional downward effects on the inflation process. This is the region of extreme diminishing marginal effectiveness where a marginal tightening of macroeconomic policies mainly affects unemployment with little impact on the inflation process.

One can think of the NAIRU, or $\bar{u}$ in Figure 1, as Friedman's (1968) concept of the "natural" rate, on the grounds that, for given institutions and stabilization policy rules, this is the rate that is "ground out" on average by markets. It may be noted, as well, that data observed in a stochastic world do not yield direct estimates of the DNAIRU, u^*. This has important implications for the methodology of estimating the Phillips curve and testing for convexity, as discussed below.

Intrinsic and Expectational Dynamics

The core version of Mark III retains the assumption that the inflation process has important myopic and forward-looking components, as in equation (7). However, an attempt has been made to distinguish between inflation inertia that arises because of overlapping wage and price contracts, which we refer to as intrinsic dynamics, and those dynamics that arise because of expectational rigidities.

The Phillips curve in the core version of Mark III is represented by equation (9).

$$\pi_t = \delta \pi_{t+1}^e + (1 - \delta)\pi_{t-1} + \gamma \frac{(u_t^* - u_t)}{(u_t - \phi_t)} + \varepsilon_t^\pi. \qquad (9)$$

The nonlinear term in the unemployment rate can be derived by assuming, as is implied by various labor market models, that the degree of real wage rigidity increases in the face of higher unemployment and market pressures for a wage decline; recall Box 6. The motivation for inflation inertia in equation (9) reflects an overlapping contracting framework where a fixed proportion of the economy's population receives nominal wage adjustments linked to lagged inflation, while the remaining proportion negotiates wage increases linked to expected future inflation.[53]

The Mark III representation of the myopic and forward-looking components model has several desirable properties. First, by incorporating intrinsic dynamics, it is consistent with the view that inflation can be costly to reduce even if agents have model-consistent expectations.[54] Second, the Mark III specification can in principle account for some differences in the structure and type of nominal inertia and real wage rigidities across countries, and hence for differences in inflation persistence across countries. Third, by separating the intrinsic and expectational dynamics, it makes it easier to isolate the implications of alternative assumptions about the formation of inflation expectations.

Proxies for Inflation Expectations

There has been some success in utilizing survey measures of inflation expectations to estimate quarterly models of the U.S. unemployment-inflation process that feature convexity.[55] Unfortunately, reliable historical survey measures of inflation expectations do not exist for all of the industrial countries. The strategy for Mark III is to use available survey measures of one-year-ahead inflation expectations data for the United States to derive an estimate of the myopic component of inflation expectations $(1 - \Phi)$. We then employ this estimate of $(1 - \Phi)$, combined with data on the yields on long-term government bonds in each country, to extract a proxy for one-

---

[52]This functional form is a slight generalization of the one employed in the TRYM model—see Australia (1996)—and is very similar to the function that was estimated in Chadha, Masson, and Meredith (1992).

[53]See Fuhrer and Moore (1995) for a derivation of a model with backward- and forward-looking components in a linear Phillips curve framework.

[54]For discussions of the analytics of disinflation in models with backward- and forward-looking components, see Buiter and Miller (1985) and Chadha, Masson, and Meredith (1992). Equation (9) includes both real and nominal rigidities. For a summary of the recent literature on the microfoundations of the Phillips curve and the importance of both nominal and real rigidities, see Ball and Mankiw (1994).

[55]Clark, Laxton, and Rose (1996) and others have shown that the Michigan Survey of one-year-ahead inflation expectations provides significant information content in quarterly inflation equations.

Box 6. Model of a Convex Phillips Curve

A very simple derivation of a nonlinear Phillips curve is presented to provide some further insight into the features of labor and goods markets that may possibly underlie its convexity. To proceed, we borrow from the framework discussed in Layard, Nickell, and Jackman (1991) and Clark and Laxton (1997). Specifically, price-setting and wage-setting behavior are characterized respectively as follows:

$$p = w + \delta_0 - \delta_1 u, \qquad (1)$$

$$w = p^e + \varphi_0 - \varphi_1 u. \qquad (2)$$

Equation (1) specifies that (the logarithm of) the price level p is set as a (constant) markup over unit labor costs, expressed in terms of the (log) wage rate w and the rate of unemployment u, which can also be related to output or capacity utilization via Okun's law. Equation (2) represents a target real wage expression in which φ_1 signifies the responsiveness of real wage demands to the level of unemployment, and p^e is the expected price level.

In the presence of nominal inertia, equation (1) can be viewed as defining a target price level (denoted with a bar), and the observed price can be assumed to adjust only gradually to the target price according to

$$\Delta p = \lambda_1(\bar{p} - p_{-1}) + \lambda_2 \Delta p_{-1}. \qquad (3)$$

The first term on the right-hand side of equation (3) represents an error-correction mechanism, while the second term introduces (higher-order) inertia in inflation ($\pi = \Delta p$) and not just the price level.

Using these three equations with $\lambda_2 = (1 - \lambda_1)$, one can derive a *linear* expectations-augmented Phillips curve that summarizes the (reduced-form) relationship between inflation and unemployment:[1]

$$\pi = \lambda_1 \pi^e + (1 - \lambda_1)\pi_{-1} + \lambda_1(\varphi_1 + \delta_1)(u^* - u), \qquad (4)$$

where expected inflation is defined by $\pi^e = p^e - p_{-1}$. Note that in equilibrium, $\pi_{-1} = \pi = \pi^e$ in conjunction with an unemployment rate equal to the DNAIRU, u^*, which coincides with the NAIRU in the linear case.[2]

---

[1]Imposing $\lambda_1 + \lambda_2 = 1$ in equation (3) translates it into an error-correction equation for *inflation* rather than the price *level*: $\Delta \pi = \lambda_1(\bar{\pi} - \pi_{-1})$; this specification implies inflation persistence, given by $1 - \lambda_1$, and allows for a non-zero (steady-state) equilibrium inflation rate where $\pi_{-1} = \pi = \bar{\pi}$.

[2]In expectational equilibrium ($p = p^e$) with nonaccelerating prices ($\Delta \pi = 0$), the equilibrium unemployment rate, or NAIRU, is given by

$$u^* = \frac{\varphi_0 + \delta_0}{\varphi_1 + \delta_1}.$$

In equation (4), the responsiveness of π to π^e, as measured by λ_1, can be regarded as the degree of nominal flexibility. The coefficient on the unemployment gap reflects both the degree of nominal flexibility and—following the discussion in Layard, Nickell, and Jackman (1991)—the degree of real rigidity $RR = (\varphi_1 + \delta_1)^{-1}$. Note that RR is high when φ_1 and δ_1 are small or when prices and wages are not very responsive to the level of unemployment. The interaction between the degrees of nominal flexibility and real rigidity determines the slope of the linear Phillips curve, reflecting the constant short-run trade-off between inflation and unemployment. For example, greater nominal flexibility (larger λ_1), other things being equal, implies a steeper Phillips curve.

Nonlinearity is introduced into the Phillips curve when the parameters that determine the short-run trade-off between inflation and unemployment are variables that change with labor market conditions. For example, if the degree of real wage rigidity is a *function* of the level of unemployment, such that $RR = h(u)$ with $h' > 0$, the Phillips curve would exhibit convexity. In the simple case where this function has the linear form $h(u) = \Lambda u - \Omega$, we can rewrite the Phillips curve as follows:

$$\pi = \lambda_1 \pi^e + (1 - \lambda_1)\pi_{-1} + \gamma\left(\frac{u^* - u}{u - \Omega/\Lambda}\right); \gamma \equiv \lambda_1/\Lambda. \quad (5)$$

Note that an increase in nominal flexibility (larger λ_1) or an increase in real flexibility (smaller Λ) raises the coefficient γ in the above expression. The motivation for assuming that the degree of real wage rigidity *increases* in the face of higher unemployment can be found in the implications of several labor market models.

For example, in incentive wage models, employers find it desirable to pay an efficiency wage greater than the market-clearing wage in order to induce effort, sustain morale, reduce turnover, avoid adverse selection problems, and so on, which places an effective *floor* (that is, asymmetry) on adjustment in real wages. To the extent that the wage floor becomes an increasingly binding constraint as unemployment rises, these models have the implication that the degree of real wage rigidity increases with the unemployment rate. Correspondingly, the "wage gap"—between the prevailing (efficiency) wage and the market clearing wage—would increase with the unemployment rate. Asymmetric wage bargaining could also have similar implications. In effect, once market rigidities vary with the level of activity and employment, the wage-price mechanism is no longer linear.

year-ahead inflation expectations for each of the industrial countries in our sample.

The exact procedure for constructing the inflation expectation proxies involves the following three steps. First, following Debelle and Laxton (1997), forward-looking measures of long-term inflation expectations are constructed for each country by subtracting a measure of the equilibrium world real interest rate from a measure of the country's long-term nominal interest rate.[56] Second, we regress the Michigan Survey measure of one-year-ahead inflation expectations for the United States[57] on lagged CPI inflation and the constructed long-term inflation expectation measure π^{LTE}. This produces an estimate of $(1 - \Phi)$ of 0.47.[58] Using this estimate of $(1 - \Phi)$, we then construct a set of one-year-ahead inflation expectation proxies for each country using the following equation.

$$\hat{\pi}^e_{t+1} = \Phi \, \pi^{LTE}_t + [1 - \Phi]\pi_{t-1}. \tag{10}$$

This empirical strategy results in highly persistent deviations between the constructed inflation expectation and observed inflation rates. Such "expectation errors" are, in principle, capable of explaining persistence in the business cycle, and, when combined with the convex Phillips curve, this empirical methodology can produce fairly large magnitudes for the cyclical level of unemployment in those countries that have experienced both high unemployment and low policy credibility.[59]

The fact that these inflation expectation proxies are based on long-term interest rates, which have long-term memory components, does not necessarily imply that agents' forecasts of inflation are irrational.[60] Because there is nothing really fundamental in a democratic system to tie down the distribution of future monetary policies—beyond the reputation of today's policymakers—it may take a considerable amount of time for rational agents to become convinced that governments are committed to low inflation.[61] Along the transition path, it may still be rational for market participants, when confronted with a new regime, to discount recent inflation performance under the new regime and to place a high weight on long moving averages of past inflation performance until it is evident that policymakers are committed to living with any adverse consequences of low inflation.[62]

Estimates of the Mark III Phillips Curve

The methodology that we employ to estimate the Mark III Phillips curve is based on estimating model-consistent measures of the labor market tightness term $(u^* - u)$ in equation (11).

$$\pi_t = \delta \hat{\pi}^e_{t+1} + [1 - \delta]\pi_{t-1} + \gamma \frac{[u^*_t - u_t]}{[u_t - \phi_t]} + \varepsilon^\pi_t. \tag{11}$$

Equation (11) can be estimated as a simple time-varying parameter model by assuming that u^*, the DNAIRU, follows a random walk. If we define an artificial variable Z_t as follows,

$$Z_t = \frac{\gamma u^*_t}{u_t - \phi_t}, \tag{12}$$

then equation (11) can be rewritten as

$$\pi_t = \delta \hat{\pi}^e_{t+1} + [1 - \delta]\pi_{t-1} + Z_t - \frac{\gamma u_t}{[u_t - \phi_t]} + \varepsilon^\pi_t. \tag{13}$$

---

[56]This first step is based on an assumption that most of the variation in long-term bond yields is a result of variation in long-term inflation expectations. The measure of the equilibrium world real interest rate term is meant to account for the trend increase (low frequency variation) in the equilibrium real interest rate that has been a result of the rise in world government debt;for details, see Debelle and Laxton (1997). Goodfriend (1993) and Barr and Campbell (1996) argue that most of the high-frequency variation in long-term bond yields is driven by inflation scares rather than by historical movements in the ex ante real rate of interest.

[57]Reliable survey measures of inflation expectations for other countries span substantially shorter time periods than the data for the United States.

[58]The standard error of this estimate is 0.18. Users of MULTIMOD may vary this parameter in simulation mode.

[59]The term "policy credibility" refers here to the speed with which inflation expectations adjust in response to announced changes in policy obxjectives for inflation.

[60]The estimation strategy employed here is considerably different from what has been employed in the recent U.S. academic literature on Phillips curves. The latter literature imposes a very strong form of the rational expectations hypothesis, where agents do not make serially correlated forecast errors even in small samples. In structural models, this extreme form of rational expectations breaks down quickly with modest amounts of uncertainty, which explains why these models are rejected overwhelmingly by less restricted time-series representations of the data. For evidence of autocorrelated forecast errors and historical regime shifts in the inflation process, see Evans and Wachtel (1993), Laxton, Ricketts, and Rose (1994), and Ricketts and Rose (1995).

[61]Recent studies focusing on the behavior of long-term interest rates suggest that market participants in some cases revise their expectations of long-term inflation very slowly in response to observed inflation performance. For example, Gagnon (1996) shows that the Fisher equation holds surprisingly well if long moving averages of past inflation are used to measure long-term inflation expectations.

[62]Using a multiple regime-switching model, Laxton, Ricketts, and Rose (1994) show that, because of historical inflation bias, it may take the monetary authorities a considerable length of time to establish credibility in a low-inflation regime and that, along the transition path, there will be a persistent period of excess supply until credibility has been established. However, in any one particular draw, inflation expectations will converge slowly and then suddenly credibility will improve when the time-series properties of the inflation process become consistent with the underlying policy fundamentals. This view of the importance of policy credibility can account for slow adjustment on the one hand, as well as for cases where long-term interest rates jump because market participants become convinced that the monetary authorities and democratic process are committed to low inflation. This can explain, for example, why it has taken a very long time for long-term inflation expectations in Canada to fall below rates in the United States, but how certain countries that appear to be committed to Economic and Monetary Union have experienced a very rapid decline in their long-term interest rate differentials with Germany.

Under the assumption that u_t^* follows a random walk, equation (13) can be estimated as a time-varying parameter model using standard Kalman filter procedures.[63] It is then straightforward to obtain estimates of u_t^* by solving equation (12) after time-varying estimates of Z_t are derived from the Kalman filtering procedure. Assuming that γ and ϕ are taken as given, the assumption that u_t^* follows a random walk implies that $Z_t = Z_{t-1} + \varepsilon_t^z$. To implement the Kalman filter routine, it is necessary to specify the signal-to-noise ratio or, more precisely in this instance, the variance of ε^z relative to the variance of ε^π. With annual data, we found that simply using the default option of unity in most econometric packages[64] produced estimates of u_t^* that were not excessively volatile.

However, before equation (13) can be estimated, it is necessary to specify a measurement equation for ϕ_t, which can be regarded as the "unemployment wall" parameter. Recall from Figure 1 that ϕ represents the lower bound on unemployment, below which the economy cannot operate regardless of the degree of excess demand. In countries where the unemployment rate has drifted upward, it seems quite plausible that ϕ has drifted upward as well; recall the discussion of asymmetric hysteresis. The specification adopted for the minimum unemployment wall is the following:

$$\phi_t = MAX\ [0,\ \bar{u}_t - 4], \qquad (14)$$

where $\bar{u}_t$ is a time-varying measure of the natural rate of unemployment. Box 7 provides a discussion of the filtering method that was used to construct the estimates of the $\bar{u}_t$ and shows the estimates of the $\bar{u}_t$. Obviously, there is considerable uncertainty about any estimates of the ϕ_t since econometricians are not likely to have any observations of unemployment rates in its neighborhood. Part of our justification for adopting the specification in equation (14) is that it implies modest convexity, or approximate linearity, of the Phillips curve in the neighborhood of the DNAIRU, u^*. In addition, this seems more attractive than setting $\phi_t = 0$, as was done in the initial application of this functional form (see Debelle and Laxton, 1997). The specification with $\phi_t = 0$ has some undesirable counterfactual properties because it would suggest that countries with extremely rigid labor markets and high unemployment rates would have lower convexity than countries with low unemployment rates and very flexible labor markets.

Table 1 provides estimates of the key parameters of the short-run Phillips curve model for the seven

---

[63]Kuttner (1992, 1994) adopts a strategy that is closest to the one we follow, but he assumes that the Phillips curve has a linear specification.

[64]The software package that was used to estimate the model was TSP.

Table 1. Phillips Curve Model

$$\pi_t = \gamma_\pi \left(\frac{u_t^* - u_t}{u_t - \phi_t} \right) + \lambda_\pi \hat{\pi}_{t+1}^e + (1 - \lambda_\pi)\pi_{t-1}$$

$\pi_t \equiv \Delta$ log price level (deflator for non-oil GNP)

$\hat{\pi}_{t+1}^e \equiv$ inflation expectation proxy

$u_t \equiv$ unemployment rate

$u_t^* \equiv$ DNAIRU

$\phi_t \equiv$ minimum short-run unemployment wall

	γ_π	λ_π	R^2	SE
Canada	0.018** (0.009)	1.00[1]	0.39	0.016
France	0.011** (0.005)	0.75** (0.24)	0.63	0.009
Germany	0.008** (0.004)	0.74** (0.30)	0.69	0.009
Italy	0.023* (0.016)	0.91** (0.37)	0.61	0.020
Japan	0.091** (0.045)	1.00[1]	0.50	0.026
United Kingdom	0.024** (0.015)	1.00[1]	0.25	0.035
United States	0.013** (0.008)	0.69** (0.30)	0.38	0.012

Note: Standard errors reported in parentheses; ** (*) indicates that estimated coefficient is significantly different from zero at the 5 percent (10 percent) significance level.

[1]Imposed value.

major industrial countries when equation (13) is estimated over a sample period that starts in 1976 and ends in 1996. Given the small number of observations in our sample and the limited number of business cycles, one should expect significant uncertainty in the parameter estimates. Because of such imprecision in estimated parameters, previous versions of MULTIMOD have reflected decisions to impose the same parameter values across countries in cases where individual country estimates were judged to be implausible.

In Table 1, the estimated parameter on the inflation expectation term (λ_π), which reflects the degree of nominal flexibility (recall Box 6), is less than one for France, Germany, Italy, and the United States, indicating that these economies may be characterized by greater nominal rigidities than Canada, Japan, and the United Kingdom, for which the estimated values exceeded one and coefficients of unity were therefore imposed. The parameter on the labor market tightness term (γ_π) to a large extent reflects the degree of real wage rigidities. The estimates of relatively low

---

Box 7. A Simple Prior-Consistent Filter for Measuring the Natural Rate

The Mark III Phillips curve embodies model-consistent estimates of the time series of u_t^* (the DNAIRU) and ϕ_t (the unemployment wall parameter) that are generated from estimates of the time series of $\bar{u}_t$, the natural rate of unemployment (also called the NAIRU). The latter are generated using a simple prior-consistent filter. The choice of this particular filter was based upon the following considerations. First, we wanted the method to be able to accommodate simple prior assumptions about how the natural rate has evolved over time. For example, for work with data from the industrial countries, we would want to allow for the possibility that the natural rate has drifted up over time. However, at the same time, we would also not want to rule out the possibility that it may have actually fallen in some countries during certain periods. Second, we wanted it to be straightforward to impose prior assumptions about the variance of the natural rate relative to the observed unemployment rate. Third, we wanted an approach that could easily incorporate information from research that has been directed at accounting for trend variation in the natural rate. These considerations ruled out many of the possible techniques and led us to specify a simple prior-consistent (PC) filter.[1]

Estimates of the natural rate from the PC filter are derived by minimizing the squared deviations of the observed unemployment rate, u_t, from the natural rate, $\bar{u}_t$, subject to a constraint that penalizes squared deviations in the change in the natural rate relative to some prior estimate of the change in the natural rate, which we denote as $\Delta\bar{u}_t^*$. Specifically, given a sample of observations that range from 1 to T, the PC filter solves for the sequence $\{\bar{u}_t\}$ that minimizes the objective function:

$$\sum_{t=1}^{T}(u_t - \bar{u}_t)^2 + \lambda_{pc}\sum_{t=2}^{T}\left[(\bar{u}_t - \bar{u}_{t-1}) - \Delta\bar{u}_t^*\right]^2.$$

The PC filter is a close cousin to the Hodrick-Prescott (HP) filter (see Hodrick and Prescott, 1981). However, by penalizing deviations from prior estimates of changes in the natural rate instead of just penalizing curvature, the PC filter has the advantage of allowing us to incorporate any priors we may have on the natural rate via the $\Delta\bar{u}_t^*$ terms.[2]

Values of the $\Delta\bar{u}_t^*$ could perhaps be obtained from structural studies of the natural rate that attempt to identify factors that can explain why the natural rate may have shifted over time.[3] However, without specific information about shifts in the natural rate, we have chosen to set the $\Delta\bar{u}_t^*$ terms to zero. This seems to be an appropriate choice for a variable like the unemployment rate that could be subject to permanent shocks but should not be expected to continue to drift upward continuously over time.

The value of λ_{pc} in the PC filter can be determined by forming priors about what would constitute a very large value of the unemployment gap compared to priors about a very large change in the natural rate of unemployment. For example, a very high value of λ_{pc} would imply an approximately constant estimate for the natural rate over the sample, while a very low value for λ_{pc} would allow the natural rate to roughly coincide with the actual unemployment rate. One way of calibrating λ_{pc} in practice is to set it at a level at which a particular pair of extreme values for the unemployment gap and the change in the natural rate would have identical effects on the value of the objective function. For most of the countries in our sample, a 5 percent unemployment gap would be a large unemployment gap,

---

[1]Univariate filters—such as the one employed here—are clearly a second-best solution to a more sophisticated structural approach that would attempt to develop model-consistent measures of the natural rate that included both deterministic and stochastic elements. However, while a preferred "structural approach" has been implemented with some success in a few industrial countries, it has been problematic for explaining trend variation in the natural rate in several other industrial countries. See Blanchard and Katz (1997).

[2]The objective function for the HP filter can be obtained by replacing $\Delta\bar{u}^*$ in the PC objective function with $\bar{u}_{t-1} - \bar{u}_{t-2}$. One problem with the HP filter is that the estimates of the trend series can be virtually useless at the end of the sample because there are very few meaningful restrictions to tie down the level of the trend series. The PC filter can be potentially more informative in cases where there is a strong prior for steady-state changes in the underlying trend series.

[3]For examples of a more structural approach to estimating the natural rate of unemployment, see Ford and Rose (1989), Adams and Coe (1990), and Layard, Nickell, and Jackman (1991).

---

values of this parameter for France and Germany suggest that these economies have relatively high degrees of downward real wage resistance. At the other extreme, Japan has a very high value of γ_π, suggesting that, of the seven major industrial countries, Japan's economy has the lowest degree of real wage rigidities. The relative responsiveness in the model of real and nominal variables to monetary shocks will depend intricately on the degrees of real and nominal

rigidities in the economy under consideration. For example, output and unemployment will respond more to monetary shocks in countries (such as Germany) that have relatively high degrees of both nominal and real rigidities than in countries (such as Japan) that have very low degrees of both nominal and real rigidities; see Box 8 for a discussion of the simulation properties of the model in response to positive and negative money supply shocks.

Estimates of the Natural Rate of Unemployment

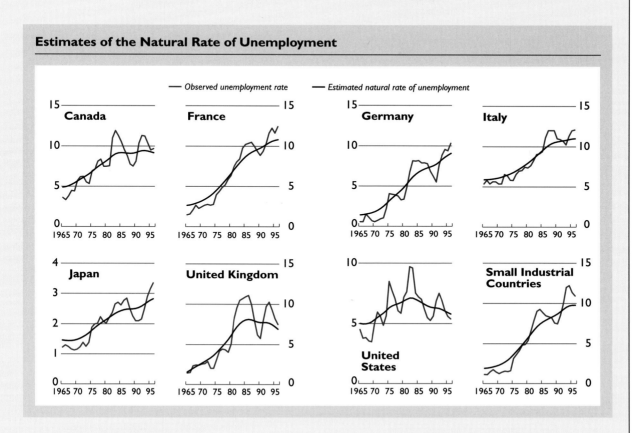

— Observed unemployment rate   — Estimated natural rate of unemployment

while a 1 percentage point annual change in the natural rate would also be considered very large. These particular extreme values make equal contributions to the PC penalty function when λ_{pc} equals 25, which is the value we have chosen to use in estimating natural rates for the core Mark III model.[4]

[4]In general, once users have identified their priors for a large value of the unemployment gap and a large change in the natural rate, they can then extract λ_{pc} from the following formula:

$$(\text{Prior for large gap})^2 =$$
$$\lambda_{pc} (\text{Prior for large change in natural rate})^2$$

The panels in the figure present estimates of the trend rate of unemployment for the industrial countries in Mark III when λ_{pc} is set at 25. According to these estimates, the natural rate of unemployment has shifted up significantly in all countries except the United States, which seems quite plausible. In addition, unlike attempts to explain the historical behavior of unemployment rates in terms of simple time trends in natural rates (see Blanchard and Quah (1989) for example), the approach taken here allows for the possibility that in some countries the upward drift in unemployment may have come to an end. For the United States, the estimates in the figure suggest that the natural rate has fallen somewhat during the 1990s.

The Dynamic Effects of Output Gaps on Unemployment

The Mark III version includes a very simple and parsimonious dynamic Okun's law equation to translate movements in the output gap $(y - \bar{y})$ into movements in the unemployment gap $(u - \bar{u})$:

$$[u_t - \bar{u}_t] = \gamma_{u1}(y_t - \bar{y}_t) + \gamma_{u2}[u_{t-1} - \bar{u}_{t-1}] + \varepsilon_t^u. \quad (15)$$

Equation (15) can be viewed as a derived demand for labor function, taking the demand for output as given.[65] The partial adjustment of unemployment

[65]Specifications of the derived demand for labor typically also include a real wage disequilibrium term, as in Bartolini, Razin, and Symansky (1995). However, the estimated parameter on this term is usually found to be fairly small compared with the role of the output gap, and this effect is ignored in Mark III.

Box 8. Asymmetries and Country-Specific Differences in the Real and Nominal Effects of Shocks

The existence of short-run capacity constraints in Mark III implies that the relative magnitudes of the real and nominal effects of shocks to aggregate demand depend on the initial position of the economy. If the economy is initially characterized by a high degree of excess supply, an increase in aggregate demand induced by a change in either monetary or fiscal policy will result in larger changes in real economic activity and unemployment in the short run, and smaller changes in prices, than if the economy is initially characterized by a high degree of excess demand. Indeed, in the limit, if the unemployment rate was at the minimum level feasible under the short-run supply curve in the model, an increase in aggregate demand would result only in inflation without any change in real activity.

The degree of asymmetry in MULTIMOD is illustrated in the table, which contrasts the effects of positive and negative money supply shocks on several countries individually. The focus is on countries that have flexible exchange rates in the base-case version of Mark III—Canada, Germany, Japan, United Kingdom, and United States. The simulations are performed on the individual country models, without taking account of international spillover and feedback effects.

The table reports the shock-minus-control results for real GDP, unemployment, the GNP deflator, and the CPI. The shocks represent positive and negative 10 percent changes in money surplus starting from conditions of full-employment equilibrium. Because the shocks are fairly large, they provide a good indication of the degree of asymmetry in the model when fairly significant movements exist along the short-run aggregate supply function. For all countries, the positive shocks have smaller short-run effects on real variables and larger short-run effects on nominal variables than the negative shocks.

Cross-country comparisons show that the effects of shocks depend on the relative degrees of nominal and real rigidities exist in the different countries. As seen in the table, for countries like Germany, where significant real and nominal rigidities exist, changes in aggregate demand can have persistent effects on real economic activity and unemployment, particularly if the shocks tend to move the economy into a position of excess supply.

The table also provides some estimates of the cumulative changes in real GDP and unemployment over the first five years of the shock. According to these measures, the degree of asymmetry is the largest in Germany and the smallest in Japan.

The Asymmetric Effects of Positive and Negative Money Supply Shocks
(Responses to 10 percent changes in the money supply)

	Year 1 +	Year 1 −	Year 2 +	Year 2 −	Year 3 +	Year 3 −	Year 4 +	Year 4 −	Year 5 +	Year 5 −	Cumulative Effect +	Cumulative Effect −
United States												
Real GDP	3.6	−4.7	2.6	−4.2	0.6	−2.4	−1.2	−0.4	−2.1	1.0	3.5	−11.0
Unemployment rate	−1.5	2.0	−1.3	2.1	−0.4	1.3	0.5	0.2	1.1	−0.5	−1.7	4.9
GNP deflator	2.2	−1.5	5.5	−3.9	8.7	−6.6	11.1	−8.9	12.5	−10.3	...	...
CPI	2.8	−2.2	5.8	−4.4	8.6	−6.7	10.8	−8.7	12.0	−10.0	...	...
Canada												
Real GDP	3.4	−4.3	2.2	−3.5	0.6	−2.1	−0.8	−0.3	−1.5	0.8	3.8	−9.3
Unemployment rate	−1.4	1.8	−1.3	2.0	−0.6	1.4	0.2	0.5	0.7	−0.2	−2.5	5.6
GNP deflator	3.8	−2.9	8.4	−6.3	11.8	−9.3	13.2	−11.2	13.0	−11.7	...	...
CPI	3.0	−2.6	6.5	−5.3	9.5	−7.8	11.3	−9.6	12.0	−10.6	...	...
Germany												
Real GDP	3.8	−4.7	4.7	−6.0	3.5	−5.3	1.6	−3.8	−0.3	−2.1	13.3	−20.0
Unemployment rate	−1.2	1.6	−1.7	2.3	−1.3	2.1	−0.6	1.5	0.1	0.8	−4.8	8.3
GNP deflator	1.0	−0.7	3.2	−2.0	5.8	−3.8	8.3	−5.7	10.5	−7.7	...	...
CPI	2.4	−2.6	3.9	−3.7	5.3	−4.4	6.8	−5.3	8.3	−6.4	...	...
Japan												
Real GDP	3.4	−3.7	3.2	−3.7	0.9	−1.3	−0.9	0.7	−1.5	1.5	5.2	−6.5
Unemployment rate	−0.2	0.2	−0.3	0.3	−0.2	0.2	0.0	0.0	0.1	−0.1	−0.6	0.6
GNP deflator	2.6	−2.6	6.5	−6.3	9.7	−9.3	11.3	−10.9	11.2	−11.0	...	...
CPI	2.8	−2.9	6.1	−6.0	9.0	−8.7	10.6	−10.3	10.9	−10.6	...	...
United Kingdom												
Real GDP	2.6	−3.3	1.5	−2.7	−0.6	−0.4	−2.0	1.6	−2.0	2.2	−0.6	−2.6
Unemployment rate	−0.8	1.1	−1.0	1.6	−0.5	1.2	0.3	0.3	0.9	−0.5	−1.1	3.6
GNP deflator	4.1	−3.5	9.5	−8.0	12.9	−11.4	13.6	−12.7	12.2	−12.1	...	...
CPI	4.4	−4.1	8.7	−7.6	11.6	−10.3	12.5	−11.7	11.9	−11.4	...	...

Note: + denotes positive 10 percent shock, and − denotes negative 10 percent shock.

gaps to output gaps embodied in equation (15) can be motivated by an assumption that it is costly to hire and fire workers, and so firms consequently adjust employment levels slowly in response to changes in the demands for their products.

Table 2 provides the econometric estimates of equation (15) under the assumption that its error term follows a first-order autoregressive process.[66] The measures of the natural rate of unemployment are obtained from the prior-consistent filter described in Box 7, and the measures of potential output are derived from a Hodrick-Prescott filter. Figure 2 provides estimates of the unemployment and output gaps that are based on these filtered estimates of the respective trend components. As can be seen in the figure, there is a striking negative correlation between the output gaps and the unemployment gaps in most countries.

The estimated parameter on the contemporaneous output gap is highly significant in all countries (see Table 2). The average value of this term across all the countries is approximately one-third, indicating that a 1 percentage point change in the excess demand gap in the goods market translates into a contemporaneous change of roughly $\frac{1}{3}$ of 1 percentage point in the difference between the observed unemployment rate and the natural rate. Because of the dynamics in equation (15), shocks that result in a persistent increase in the output gap would result in a continuing rise in the unemployment gap over time.

There are considerable differences across countries in the responses of unemployment gaps to output gaps. For example, the coefficients on the output gap are considerably smaller for Japan and Italy than for the other countries. For Japan, this presumably reflects implicit contracts between firms and workers that reduce the variability of unemployment.[67]

---

[66]The model was estimated this way because there was significant residual autocorrelation when the model was estimated with ordinary least squares in a few countries. This autocorrelation is probably a result of inconsistencies in the filtered estimates of the natural rate and potential output. In the future it would be preferable to develop model-consistent measures of these trend variables in a larger system that embodies equation (15).

[67]The relatively low parameter estimate on the output gap for Italy presumably is not attributable to extremely low variability in the underlying unemployment rate. One possibility is that Italy has had larger shocks to the natural rate of unemployment than Japan and that the simple univariate filter that is being used to estimate potential output fails to capture the direct link from changes in the natural rate to potential output. As a consequence, we would expect that the parameter estimate on the output gap may be biased downward, and this can perhaps account for why the model doesn't fit nearly as well for Italy as it does for the other countries. In future work, we hope to develop system estimates of potential output and the natural rate that will alleviate any problems of this type.

Table 2. Unemployment Equations

$(u_t - \bar{u}_t) = \gamma_{u1} (y_t - \bar{y}_t) + \gamma_{u2}(u_{t-1} - \bar{u}_{t-1})$

$\bar{u} \equiv$ estimate of the natural rate

$\bar{y} \equiv$ estimate of potential output

	γ_{u1}	γ_{u2}	R^2	SE
Canada	−0.42** (0.04)	0.32** (0.09)	0.85	0.382
France	−0.30** (0.06)	0.44** (0.16)	0.68	0.354
Germany	−0.33** (0.07)	0.18 (0.21)	0.64	0.496
Italy	−0.09** (0.06)	0.79** (0.25)	0.52	0.507
Japan	−0.06** (0.02)	0.49** (0.16)	0.71	0.125
United Kingdom	−0.33** (0.05)	0.69** (0.09)	0.86	0.476
United States	−0.42** (0.04)	0.21** (0.09)	0.85	0.352

Note: Standard errors reported in parentheses; ** indicates that estimated coefficient is significantly different from zero at the 5 percent significance level.

The CPI Equations and Import Price Pass-Through

The Mark II version of MULTIMOD included two broad measures of inflation—the rates of change of the GNP deflator and the absorption deflator—but it did not include measures based on the consumer price index (*CPI*). Consequently, it was difficult to compare model simulation results with the conventional headline measures of inflation, which typically focus on the *CPI*. The price index closest to the *CPI* in the previous version of MULTIMOD was the absorption deflator; and because its behavior is considerably different for many countries than headline *CPI*-based measures of inflation, it was a source of confusion in some instances. Accordingly, to make simulation results easier to relate to the *World Economic Outlook* and numbers reported in the popular press, the Mark III version of MULTIMOD includes explicit models for the *CPI*. Among other things, this makes it possible to include the rate of change of the *CPI* in monetary policy reaction functions for certain countries that have explicit inflation targets.

In the context of specifying a *CPI* equation, it is important to pay close attention to the degree of exchange-rate pass-through, recognizing that

Figure 2. Unemployment and Output Gaps

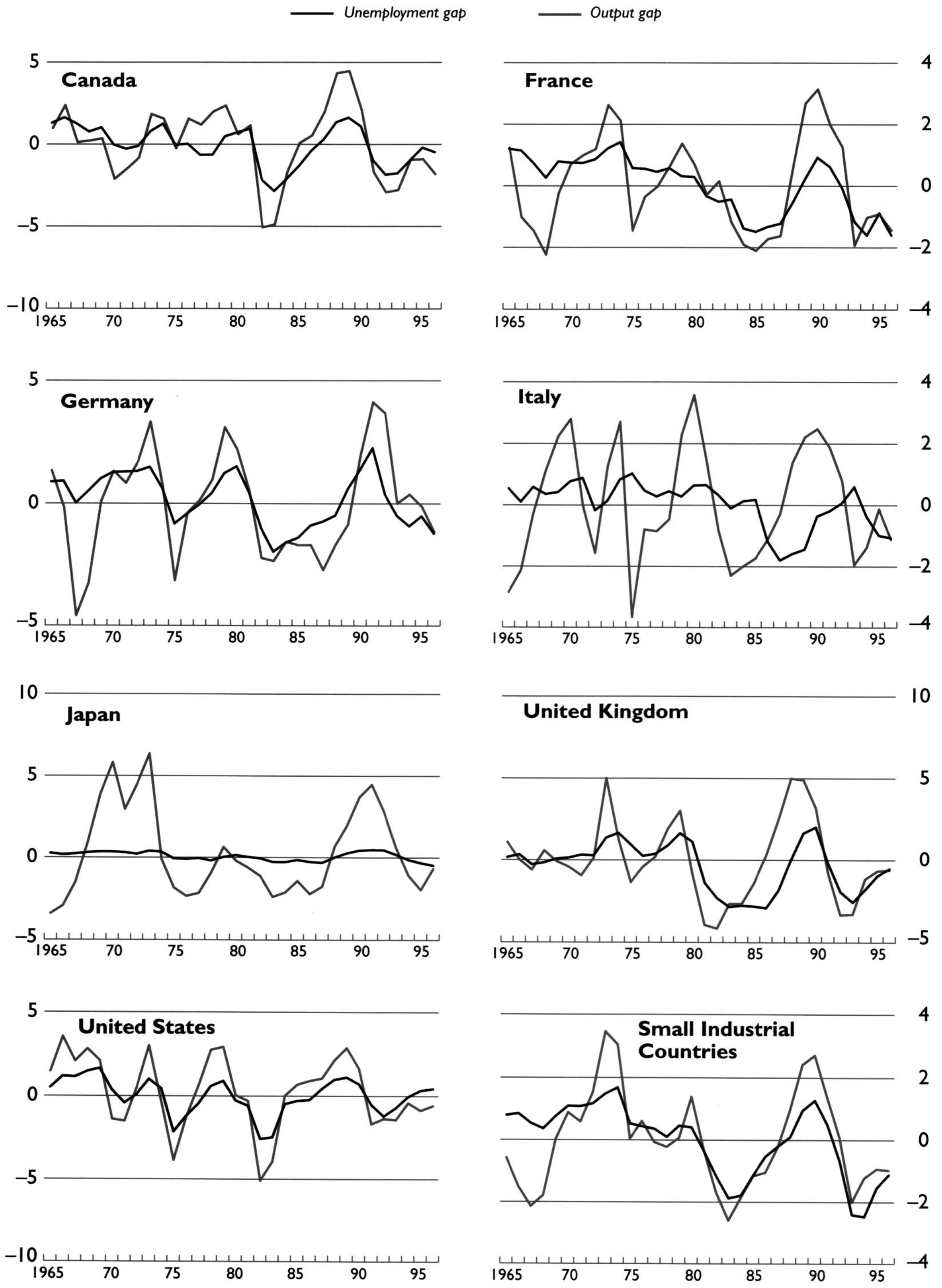

— Unemployment gap   — Output gap

Canada

France

Germany

Italy

Japan

United Kingdom

United States

Small Industrial Countries

Table 3. CPI Equations

$\Delta \log (CPI_t) = \gamma_{c1} \Delta \log (PIM_t) + \gamma_{c2} \Delta \log (PGNP_t) + (1 - \gamma_{c1} - \gamma_{c2}) \Delta \log (CPI_{t-1})$

Estimation period: 1973–96

	γ_{c1}	γ_{c2}	η_{PIM}^{LR}	R^2	SE	DW
Canada	0.09 (0.06)	0.59** (0.11)	0.13	0.88	0.112	2.32
France	0.13** (0.03)	0.82** (0.14)	0.14	0.97	0.007	1.80
Germany	0.16** (0.04)	0.56** (0.11)	0.22	0.87	0.007	1.76
Italy	0.06* (0.04)	0.85** (0.09)	0.06	0.98	0.009	2.20
Japan	0.07** (0.02)	0.79** (0.05)	0.08	0.98	0.008	1.65
United Kingdom	0.14** (0.03)	0.74** (0.05)	0.16	0.97	0.009	2.46
United States	0.06* (0.04)	0.98** (0.16)	0.06	0.90	0.010	1.53

Note: Standard errors reported in parentheses; ** (*) indicates that estimated coefficient is significantly different from zero at the 5 percent (10 percent) significance level. $\eta_{PIM}^{LR} \equiv$ long-run elasticity of the CPI with respect to import prices.

MULTIMOD is regularly subjected to shocks that affect exchange rates. The remainder of this section presents estimated short- and long-term elasticities that are obtained from reduced-form time-series relationships. To help evaluate the plausibility of these econometric estimates, we also present information on import coefficients derived from input-output tables.

The *CPI* specification in Mark III includes aggregate import prices (*PIM*), domestically produced goods prices (*PGDP*), and a lagged dependent variable to allow for partial adjustment of prices at the retail level. The equations were estimated in first differences because the sample period data did not provide evidence that the *CPI* was cointegrated with the levels of aggregate measures of import prices and the GDP deflator. The lack of a level condition in the *CPI* equation is not likely to cause any problems with the internal macro consistency of MULTIMOD's structure because the level of the *CPI* does not—and is not intended to—feed back on the rest of the model's structure.

The estimated equations for the *CPI* are reported in Table 3. The coefficients on the GNP deflator are highly significant for all countries, and in all cases except Canada the estimated parameters on the import price deflator are significantly greater than zero at the 90 percent confidence level. The equations in-dicate that there is generally fairly rapid pass-through from both import prices and producer prices to the *CPI*, but as may be seen by comparing columns 1 and 3, in some cases the long-run elastic-

Table 4. Estimated Effects on the CPI of a 1 Percent Increase in Import Price

	Estimates from Input-Output Tables[1]		Econometric Estimates	
	Direct effects[2]	Total effects[3]	Short run[4]	Long run[4]
Canada	0.10	0.21	0.08	0.13
France	0.09	0.22	0.13	0.14
Germany	0.10	0.22	0.15	0.22
Italy	0.06	0.20	0.06	0.06
Japan	0.02	0.11	0.06	0.08
United Kingdom	0.15	0.30	0.14	0.16
United States	0.07	0.10	0.06	0.06

[1]The input-output estimates are based on data for 1990 in all countries except Italy, for which they are based on data for 1985.

[2]Based on direct import contents of final goods.

[3]Reflects direct import contents of both intermediate and final goods; see main text.

[4]Estimates reported in Table 3.

ity of the *CPI* with respect to import prices is quite different from the short-run elasticity.

As can also be seen in Table 3, the parameter estimates on the import deflator are not very precisely estimated in some cases. To judge whether or not the estimated degree of import price pass-through is realistic, one should compare the short- and long-run price elasticities with simple estimates that one can compute from the input-output tables compiled by the Organization for Economic Cooperation and Development..

Table 4 reports some input-output–based estimates of import-price pass-through for the aggregate consumption deflator under two assumptions.[68] The calculations in the first column take account only of

the direct import content of final goods, assuming that there is complete pass-through for direct imports but ignoring the effects of higher import costs on the prices of intermediate goods and, hence, the associated indirect effects on the prices of final goods. The calculations in the second column include the latter indirect effects, assuming full pass-through of higher prices at each stage of processing, with no changes in unit profit margins and unit labor costs. The econometric estimates of the short-run and long-run import price elasticities from the equations estimated in Table 3 are also reported in Table 4. The econometric estimates of the long-run import price elasticities (column 4) are generally smaller than the simple measures of full import price pass-through based on the input-output tables (column 2), but the two sets of estimates have reasonably consistent orders of magnitude. Accordingly, it was decided to employ the econometric estimates in Mark III.

---

[68]These estimates are based on the latest available input-output tables; see the notes to Table 4.

V Consumption and Saving Behavior: A Life-Cycle Perspective

As emphasized in the introduction of this paper, one of MULTIMOD's most important functions is to assist with the IMF's multilateral surveillance over the policies of its members. Among other considerations, MULTIMOD has frequently been used to analyze the implications of changes in fiscal policies. In this context, it is now widely recognized that the analysis of fiscal policy in any macroeconometric model depends critically on the specification of consumption and saving behavior.

Following Keynes (1936), the view that changes in government deficits tended to have first-order effects on the level of economic activity became part of mainstream macroeconomic doctrine for several decades. However, the Keynesian framework was significantly challenged during the 1970s, partly in association with the rational expectations revolution, which generated a revival of the classical Ricardian view of government deficits.[69] From the Ricardian perspective, changes in government debt should have little or no real effects on economic activity, reflecting the view that forward-looking, rational agents would revise intertemporal consumption and saving decisions to offset the implications of changes in the intertemporal pattern of public sector consumption and saving behavior (that is, changes in government deficits).

Consistent with the rational expectations hypothesis that underlies the modern Ricardian view of fiscal policy, MULTIMOD assumes that economic agents behave in a forward-looking manner based on model-consistent (rational) expectations. It also recognizes, however, that the sensitivity of private saving behavior to a change in the public deficit depends importantly on factors other than the nature of expectations. In this context, MULTIMOD Mark III incorporates important changes (compared with Mark II) in the specification of consumption and saving behavior, which now reflect an explicit life-cycle dimension. While retaining the basic framework of forward-looking optimizing behavior, the

Mark III specification allows us to explore the implications of the life-cycle paradigm, as well as other relevant considerations such as liquidity constraints (capital market imperfections) for the effectiveness of fiscal policy.

This section describes the theoretical framework and empirical estimates that underlie the specification of life-cycle consumption and saving behavior in MULTIMOD Mark III. It also examines the macroeconomic implications of such behavior for closed and small open economies by comparing a neoclassical paradigm in which agents are characterized as disconnected generations with life-cycle features to a classical (Ricardian) paradigm that views agents as dynastic families. An analytical framework that nests these two alternative views is developed on the basis of an extended version of Blanchard's (1985) overlapping-agents model. From the neoclassical perspective,[70] the analysis shows that changes in public saving can have considerable effects on the level of national saving, with implications for interest rates and asset accumulation. To estimate the quantitative importance of these life-cycle considerations for the effects of deficit finance on real interest rates, the capital stock, and net foreign assets, the model is calibrated to actual age-earnings profiles.

In the presence of life-cycle saving behavior, the rate of saving may vary significantly over time and across individuals, depending on where agents are within their respective life cycles. Younger agents expecting a rising earnings profile may choose to borrow and consume against their permanent income, which may initially exceed current income. At middle age, agents enjoying a relatively higher level of earnings may choose to accumulate assets and save for their eventual retirement. Upon reaching retirement, individuals may tend to run down their assets (dissave) in order to maintain a given level of consumption in the face of declining labor income.

To add an empirical content to this life-cycle dimension of the analysis, the model first incorporates

---

[69]The revival of the classical view and the Ricardian equivalence proposition was led by Barro (1974). See Barro (1989) for a more recent review.

[70]The seminal paper is Diamond (1965); see Persson (1985) for open economy extensions. See Bernheim (1989) for a more recent review of the neoclassical approach to budget deficits.

a general specification of the relationship between individual earnings profiles and age. In particular, disposable labor income is assumed to generally increase with age as a worker gains experience and seniority before earnings level off and eventually decline with retirement. To calibrate the model, the time profile of labor income is estimated using earnings and employment data across different age groups in the United States.[71] Using the ensuing calibration, the parameters describing the behavior of aggregate consumption are estimated, and the dynamic effects of fiscal policy on interest rates and the accumulation of capital or net foreign assets in a life-cycle context can then be simulated.

In terms of their fiscal implications, life-cycle considerations tend to *augment* the real effects of government debt on the economy (see Faruqee, Laxton, and Symansky, 1997). With no altruistic link between generations, an increase in the fiscal deficit is not fully offset by an increase in private saving, as a share of the debt burden falls on future generations whose marginal propensities to save presently are zero. With life-cycle (eventually declining) earnings and retirement, agents further discount the impact of future tax liabilities from an increase in public debt since the prospective tax base increasingly shifts to future generations with higher taxable incomes.

In a primarily closed economy, the resultant upward pressure on interest rates from an increase in government debt tends to crowd out investment and retard the rate of capital accumulation. In a small open economy, the decline in domestic saving is manifested in a crowding out of net exports and a greater reliance on foreign borrowing. In either case, the increase in current consumption takes place at the expense of lower living standards in the future, whether through a lower level of the capital stock or higher foreign claims on future output.

These results are in sharp contrast to the classical Ricardian view of government deficits. From a Ricardian perspective, the economic consequences of public debt and deficits should be minimal. According to the government's own (intertemporal) budget constraint, deficit financing represents a change only in the timing of taxes, while the present value of taxes remains unaffected, given public expenditure. Thus, the future taxes implied by higher government debt negate the benefits of any current reduction in taxes, leaving consumer demand unchanged. In the case of higher government spending, the increased deficit implies an increase in the present value of tax liabilities, which would act to lower current consumption. In either case, an increase in the budget

deficit should be met with an increase in private saving, offsetting or diminishing the effects of lower public saving on aggregate saving and the economy.

The disparate implications of budget deficits within the Ricardian and Neoclassical paradigms stem from their contrasting views of the intergenerational link between individuals. In contrast to the life-cycle view, the Ricardian approach views agents as dynastic families, where current generations are closely linked (through a bequest motive) to their descendants. With stronger intergenerational ties, individuals are more likely to internalize the implications of the government's intertemporal budget constraint and the prospect of higher taxes in the future.[72] With dynastic saving behavior, a form of Say's law would hold for fiscal deficits, wherein an increase in the supply of government bonds (that is, deficit finance) would be met by a corresponding increase in demand (that is, private saving) at an unchanged price (interest rate). In that case, the choice between tax and deficit finance becomes irrelevant (that is, Ricardian equivalence holds) and changes in government debt are neutral in their effects on the economy.

The issue regarding the validity of Ricardian equivalence is part of an ongoing and contentious debate in which no clear consensus has emerged. The empirical evidence on the effects of fiscal deficits and other matters (for example, bequests) related to the Ricardian debate has, thus far, consisted of mixed results rather than definitive conclusions.[73] Many of the empirical tests suffer from low power, unable to reject either Ricardian equivalence *or* its failure in favor of the corresponding alternative. Consequently, the findings of various studies tend to correlate closely with how the empirical tests are structured—that is, which proposition is taken as the null hypothesis. From a policy perspective, however, formulating policy based on the "wrong" hypothesis can lead to serious welfare consequences. In that sense, assuming that Ricardian equivalence fails may be the more appropriate starting point given that the costs of inappropriate policies may significantly outweigh those associated with irrelevant policies. In other words, the welfare costs of inappropriately failing to take fiscal actions when fiscal policies matter (based on a false acceptance of Ricardian equivalence) are likely to exceed the welfare costs of erroneously adjusting fiscal policy when fis-

---

[71]See Jappelli and Pagano (1989) for an international comparison of age-earnings profiles (and capital market imperfections).

[72]See Bernheim and Bagwell (1988) for a critical review on the dynastic approach.

[73]In a survey of empirical tests for Ricardian equivalence, Seater (1993) claims that the evidence is supportive of the equivalence proposition; at the same time, however, he acknowledges that the results of various studies correlate closely with the political leanings of the investigator (p.184). See Barro (1989) and Bernheim (1989) for opposing interpretations of the empirical evidence.

cal policy is ineffective (based on a false rejection of Ricardian equivalence).

The Basic Model

Following Blanchard (1985), we consider an economy where agents have finite planning horizons (that is, a positive probability of death). In the case of dynasties, the probability of death represents the likelihood that the family line will end; in the case of overlapping agents who are disconnected from each other (that is, no bequest motive), the probability of death is related to an individual's life expectancy.

Specifically, consider an economy populated by finitely lived agents, each facing a constant probability p of dying at each moment in time, and a planning horizon (that is, the expected time until death) given by $1/p$.[74] Also, at each point in time a new generation (or dynasty) is born of relative size normalized to p, so that the size of the population remains constant. Specifically, the number of surviving agents from a cohort born at time s and remaining at time t is equal to $pe^{-p(t-s)}$, leaving the total number of agents—aggregating over all existing cohorts (indexed by s)—constant and normalized to unity.[75]

Consumption

Agents are assumed to maximize expected utility over their lifetimes subject to a budget constraint.[76] Specifically, the evolution of financial wealth $w(s,t)$ for an individual or household is determined by its saving, defined as the difference between income and consumption:

$$\dot{w}(s,t) = [r(t) + p]w(s,t) + y(s,t) - \tau(s,t) - c(s,t), \quad (16)$$

where r is the interest rate, y is labor income, τ is taxes (net of transfers), and c is consumption, all expressed in real terms (units of consumption).[77] In a small open economy, the real interest rate is also assumed to be exogenous and fixed at the world real rate of interest. Ignoring for now capital market imperfections and liquidity constraints, optimal consumption should be based on an agent's permanent income. Explicitly, solving the dynamic optimization problem facing consumers, individual consumption is given by[78]

$$c(s,t) = (\theta + p)[w(s,t) + h(s,t)], \quad (17)$$

where θ is the rate of time preference in utility, and $h(s,t)$ is a measure of an agent's human wealth—equal to the present value of future labor income.[79]

Aggregating over all agents,[80] total consumption as a function of (financial and human) wealth can be expressed as follows:

$$C = (\theta + p)[W + H], \quad (18)$$

where uppercase letters denote economy-wide aggregates. Financial wealth W equals the sum of domestic equity K, bond holdings B, and in an open economy, holdings of net foreign assets F:

$$W \equiv K + B + F. \quad (19)$$

As for aggregate human wealth, its definition depends on the treatment of agents as dynasties or disconnected generations of individuals.

The Behavior of Dynastic Households

When households represent dynasties rather than (disconnected) generations, an individual's planning horizon may far exceed his or her own actual lifetime, as people internalize the welfare and circumstances of their descendants as their own. Correspondingly, human wealth is expressed in terms of the disposable income stream available to the dynastic household. As dynasties themselves do not possess any life-cycle dimension, members from different households (regardless of age) can be treated identically. Consistent with this representative-agent framework, income and taxes are *not* generation-specific (that is, $y(s,t) = Y(t)$, $\tau(s,t) = T(t)$). Consequently, the dynamics for total human wealth under a dynastic interpretation can be written (dropping the time index) as[81]

---

[74]See Blanchard (1985). If the probability of death goes to zero, agents have infinite horizons.

[75]The case of population (and productivity) growth is addressed later.

[76]Labor supply is taken to be inelastically supplied. Hence, the labor-leisure decision is not part of the consumer's optimization problem. See Ludvigson (1996) for a recent paper on fiscal policy effects with endogenous labor supply.

[77]The term $pw(s,t)$ in the dynamic budget constraint reflects the efficient operation of the life insurance or annuities market. See Yaari (1965) or Blanchard (1985).

[78]This result assumes logarithmic utility. The case of constant relative risk aversion (CRRA utility) (see also Blanchard, 1985) and the implications of different intertemporal substitution elasticities are explored in Faruqee, Laxton, and Symansky (1997).

[79]For a given (world) real interest rate, individual human wealth can be written as

$$h(s,t) = \int_t^\infty [y(s,v) - \tau(s,v)]e^{-(r+p)(v-t)}dv.$$

[80]To derive aggregate variables, we simply sum over all existing generations (or dynasties). Specifically, aggregate variables, denoted by uppercase letters, are derived by integrating over all existing cohorts or generations (indexed by s):

$$X(t) \equiv \int_{-\infty}^t x(s,t)pe^{-p(t-s)}ds.$$

[81]To simplify notation, the time arguments in the equations have been dropped in the text, except where potential ambiguities may arise. The time index is reintroduced in the tables.

$$\dot{H} = (r + p)H - [Y - T]. \tag{20}$$

Under this representative agent assumption, household income (and taxes) is independent of age and can grow indefinitely with long-run productivity growth. With a growing taxable income base over time, agents belonging to dynastic households remain sensitive to changes in future tax burdens falling on themselves *or* their descendants. Indeed, Evans (1991) shows that this variant of the model obeys approximate Ricardian equivalence, and that variations in planning horizons (that is, changes in the birth and death rate p) do not substantially alter this basic property of the model. This result, however, rests crucially on the assumption of dynastic rather than life-cycle behavior, as will become apparent below.

The Life-Cycle Behavior of Disconnected Generations

For the case in which agents represent overlapping generations of individuals (rather than dynasties) disconnected from one another, the planning horizon reflects an individual's expected life span, during which time life-cycle considerations are relevant. To capture these features, the basic framework can be modified to incorporate a time profile of labor income that conforms to empirical observations, rising with age and experience when individuals are young, before eventually declining with retirement when they are old.[82]

To introduce a concave earnings profile over an individual's lifetime, we assume that the income $y(s,t)$ accruing to an individual from generation s at time t, as a proportion of aggregate labor income $Y(t)$, can be expressed using age-dependent weights determined by the sum of two exponential functions (to allow for aggregation) as follows:[83]

$$y(s,t) = [a_1 e^{-\alpha_1(t-s)} + a_2 e^{-\alpha_2(t-s)}]Y(t);$$
$$a_1 > 0, \; a_2 < 0, \; \alpha_1, \alpha_2 > 0. \tag{21}$$

The first exponential term, which decays over time, can be interpreted as the effects of the gradually declining endowment of labor (that is, gradual retirement), which is inelastically supplied. The second exponential term, which rises (toward zero) over time, can be interpreted as reflecting the relative productivity and wage gains associated with increased experience (age).

With age-dependent income and lifetime-earnings profiles, the dynamics governing aggregate human wealth are modified accordingly, with equation (20) replaced by

$$H = \beta H_1 + (1 - \beta)H_2, \tag{22}$$
$$\dot{H_1} = (r + p + \alpha_1)H_1 - [Y - T], \tag{23}$$

and

$$\dot{H_2} = (r + p + \alpha_2)H_2 - [Y - T]. \tag{24}$$

Human wealth, measuring the present value of future disposable labor income, is now expressed as the sum of two components, reflecting the concave nature of an individual's income over the life cycle.

As will be shown explicitly later, the real effects of government debt on the economy tend to be larger in the case of disconnected generations than in the case of dynastic households. The basic intuition can be seen by comparing equation (20) with equations (23) and (24). In the life-cycle case, by further increasing the wedge (via the α terms) between the public discount rate (r) and private discount rate beyond the wedge resulting from finite horizons ($p > 0$),[84] the model with age-dependent income suggests that the choice between tax financing and deficit financing will have more significant consequences for national consumption and saving.[85] A fall in, say, current taxes has future tax implications in each case, but in the life-cycle case the burden partly falls on future (disconnected) generations, who also will tend to have higher taxable incomes. Hence, in this case, changes in the intertemporal pattern of public saving and consumption behavior will not be negated by fully offsetting changes in private consumption and saving behavior.

The Small Open Economy Case

The small open economy is assumed to be a price taker in the world market for goods and capital; hence, consumption is expressed in terms of a single

---

[82]Blanchard (1985) examines the case of declining individual income profiles; the more realistic case of nonmonotonic (concave) earnings profiles is mentioned only in passing (footnote 75). Both cases introduce a saving-for-retirement motive and open up the possibility that the economy may be dynamically inefficient (that is, may overaccumulate capital).

[83]As discussed later, the parameters in equation (21) are chosen such that the weighting function is assumed to be nonnegative and initially increasing; by an adding-up constraint, we also require that

$$\frac{a_1 p}{\alpha_1 + p} + \frac{a_2 p}{\alpha_2 + p} = 1.$$

[84]Integrating up equation (23) yields the definition of the human wealth component H_1:

$$H_1(t) \equiv \int_t^\infty [Y(v) - T(v)]e^{-(r+p+\alpha_1)(v-t)}dv,$$

where the following boundary condition is assumed to be satisfied: $\lim_{v \to \infty} H_1(v)e^{-(r+p+\alpha_1)} = 0$; H_2 is derived equivalently from equation (24). Hence, disposable labor income is effectively discounted at a rate that depends on $r + p + \alpha_1$ and $r + p + \alpha_2$.

[85]Another critical parameter affecting the degree of debt nonneutrality is the elasticity of intertemporal substitution, which determines the sensitivity of consumption to changes in interest rates. See Faruqee, Laxton, and Symansky (1997) for a discussion.

internationally traded good (numeraire) whose price is taken as given. In a closed economy (see next subsection), specifying the behavior of consumption and saving given output and technology is sufficient to pin down investment. But in an open economy with international capital mobility, domestic investment is not constrained to equal domestic saving. Thus, to complete our characterization of the national accounts, we need to specify explicitly an investment function and also to describe the public sector and external accounts.

In specifying investment behavior, it is assumed that domestic firms can freely borrow at the (exogenous) world real interest rate. With (convex) installation costs of capital,[86] the investment decision can be derived as having a simple neoclassical specification:

$$I = (q - 1 + \delta)K, \tag{25}$$

where I is gross investment (excluding installation costs), K is the domestic capital stock, δ is the rate of depreciation of capital, and q is the (shadow) value of an additional unit of capital (related to Tobin's q). Total investment expenditure $\tilde{I}$ is given by the sum of gross investment plus adjustment or installation costs A:

$$\tilde{I} = I + A. \tag{26}$$

Domestic investment is independent of domestic saving and consumption behavior. In other words, with the ability to borrow and lend freely at a given world real rate of interest, a small open economy will choose an investment rule that is *separable* from its consumption behavior (Fisherian separability).[87] Net investment—defined as gross investment net of depreciation—determines the incremental change in the domestic capital stock:

$$\dot{K} = I - \delta K, \tag{27}$$

where again δ is the (constant) rate of depreciation or obsolescence for capital.

As for the public sector, it is assumed that government expenditures G are financed either through (lump-sum) taxation T or the issuance of govern-

ment debt B. Debt accumulation and the government's dynamic budget constraint is given by

$$\dot{B} = rB + G - T, \tag{28}$$

where B is the stock of public debt. In equation (28), the primary deficit plus interest payments on the existing stock determines the government's bond-financing requirements and the corresponding rate of debt issue.

Using national accounting identities, the current account can be expressed in terms of income, saving, and absorption. Domestic production (GDP) is given by $f(K)$, which is a concave, twice-differentiable aggregate production function (labor L normalized to 1),[88] and national income (GNP) is defined by GDP plus net interest income (factor payments) from abroad:

$$GNP = f(K) + rF. \tag{29}$$

In turn, national saving S equals national income less consumption (public and private):

$$S = GNP - C - G. \tag{30}$$

Turning to the external accounts, the difference between domestic production and absorption equals the trade balance NX (that is, net exports):

$$f(K) - C - G - \tilde{I} = NX. \tag{31}$$

The current account CA is the difference between national income and absorption (or between saving and investment):

$$CA = NX + rF = S - \tilde{I}. \tag{32}$$

Since the gap between income and expenditure must be met by international lending or borrowing, the current account also reflects changes in the stock of net foreign assets:

$$\dot{F} = CA. \tag{33}$$

Table 5 summarizes the basic equations and laws of motion for the discrete-time version of the model in a small open economy when individuals exhibit life-cycle behavior. Replacing the discrete-time analogue of equations (22) – (24) in the table with that of equation (20) would characterize the model under the dynastic assumption.

In the life-cycle case, the departure from Ricardian equivalence can be substantial. In a small open economy, these effects tend to be reflected through the net foreign asset position rather than through in-

---

[86]Following Lucas (1967) and Treadway (1969), installation costs are quadratic in the deviation of the investment-capital ratio from its steady-state value:

$$A = \frac{\chi}{2}\left[\frac{I}{K} - (\delta + g + n)\right]^2 K,$$

where g is the long-run growth rate, n is the long-run rate of population growth, and χ is a scale parameter in the adjustment cost function. For now, we consider the case where $g = n = 0$; population and productivity growth are introduced later. For convenience, we assume $\chi = 1$ throughout this section. Investment behavior is discussed more fully in Section VI.

[87]See also Turnovsky (1996) for a similar small open economy model (with Fisherian separability), but in the context of endogenous growth.

[88]Assuming that $F(K,L)$ is homogeneous-of-degree-one in its arguments, we can write the production function as $LF(K/L,1) = f(K)[\equiv F(K,1)]$ at $L = 1$. Also, the following conditions are assumed to apply to guarantee the existence of an interior steady-state solution: $0 \leq \lim_{k\to\infty} f'(K) \leq r + \delta \leq \lim_{k\to 0} f'(K) \leq \infty$. Strict concavity of $f(K)$—an increasing function—guarantees uniqueness.

**Table 5. Small Open Economy Model:
Behavioral Equations and Laws of Motion**

$$C_t = (\theta + p)[W_t + H_t]$$

$$I_t = (q_t - 1 + \delta)K_{t-1}$$

$$\Delta K_t = I_t - \delta K_{t-1}$$

$$\Delta B_t = rB_{t-1} + G_t - T_t$$

$$\Delta F_t = rF_{t-1} + f(K_t) - C_t - G_t - [I_t + A_t]$$

$$H_t = \beta H_{1t} + (1 - \beta)H_{2t}$$

$$\Delta H_{1t} = (r + p + \alpha_1)H_{1t-1} - [Y_t - T_t]$$

$$\Delta H_{2t} = (r + p + \alpha_2)H_{2t-1} - [Y_t - T_t]$$

$$\Delta q_{t+1} = (r + \delta)q_t - \frac{I_t}{K_{t-1}}(q_t - 1) + \frac{A_t}{K_{t-1}} - f'(K_t)$$

**Table 6. Closed Economy Model:
Behavioral Equations and Laws of Motion**

$$C_t = (\theta + p)[W_t + H_t]$$

$$I_t = (q_t - 1 + \delta)K_{t-1}$$

$$\Delta K_t = f(K_t) - C_t - G_t - A_t - \delta K_{t-1}$$

$$\Delta B_t = r_t B_{t-1} + G_t - T_t$$

$$H_t = \beta H_{1t} + (1 - \beta)H_{2t}$$

$$\Delta H_{1t} = (r_t + p + \alpha_1)H_{1t-1} - [Y_t - T_t]$$

$$\Delta H_{2t} = (r_t + p + \alpha_2)H_{2t-1} - [Y_t - T_t]$$

$$\Delta q_{t+1} = \left[(r_t + \delta) - \frac{I_t}{K_{t-1}}\right](q_t - 1) + \frac{1}{2}(q_t - 1)^2$$

$$r_t = f'(K_t) - \delta$$

---

terest rates and the capital stock. The appendix illustrates the dynamic effects of fiscal policy on a small open economy in the context of life-cycle consumption behavior.

The Closed Economy Case

The discussion thus far has considered the case of a fixed world real interest rate faced by a price-taking small open economy. However, in the context of global shocks (for example, changes in public debt across countries), one might expect the world real interest rate to be affected and to change over time. This phenomenon can be incorporated into the same basic framework by noting that the world as a whole is a closed economy and introducing an endogenous real interest rate to be determined by tastes, technology, and policies.

In a closed economy, domestic saving must equal investment in the absence of international capital flows (that is, zero current account). Hence, the rate of capital accumulation will depend on preferences, or on the willingness of households to forgo current consumption (save), as well as on the return to investment as determined by technology. To ensure that the level of saving equals investment, the domestic real interest rate $r(t)$ must adjust to equate the supply and demand for these funds. Under profit maximization by firms, the real interest rate must also equal the *net* marginal product of capital (that is, net of depreciation):

$$r(t) = f'(K(t)) - \delta. \tag{34}$$

As before, net investment—defined as gross investment net of depreciation—determines the incre-

mental change in the capital stock. But now, in a closed economy, domestic investment is equal to domestic saving. Hence, capital stock dynamics can be written as follows:

$$\dot{K} = f(K) - C - G - A - \delta K. \tag{35}$$

The rate of capital accumulation is determined by that portion of *GDP* (=*GNP*) that is saved or set aside after accounting for private and public consumption, capital depreciation, and installation costs.[89]

The equations characterizing the closed economy are presented in discrete time in Table 6 under the life-cycle interpretation. In comparison with Table 5, for a closed economy, net foreign assets and the current account are identically zero. Also the real interest rate in Table 6 carries a time argument.[90] The modification to incorporate dynastic households into a closed economy follows in exactly the same way as in the small open economy version of the model.

Extensions

Liquidity Constraints

The overlapping-generations framework can be extended to consider the case where capital market

---

[89]In the case of public investment, the model would need to be revised to include the contribution of the public sector to the domestic capital stock.

[90]With a time-varying rate of interest, the present value of labor income that comprises human wealth is given by

$$H(t) \equiv \int_t^\infty [Y(v) - T(v)]e^{-\int_t^v (r(z)+p)dz}dv.$$

Differentiating this expression with respect to time yields the dynamic equation for human wealth shown in Table 6.

imperfections preclude some agents from always borrowing against their future incomes. In particular, it is assumed that younger generations with insufficient collateral in the form of financial wealth are initially denied access to credit markets and, hence, are left to consume out of current resources. Assuming that a generation "graduates" out of this pool just as another is born into it, a fixed proportion λ of liquidity-constrained individuals exists in the economy. For these current-income consumers, consumption is constrained by current disposable income: $c(s,t) = y(s,t) - \tau(s,t)$, where $y(s,t)$, $c(s,t)$, and $\tau(s,t)$ are labor income, consumption, and taxes for a given generation s at time t.

Consequently, overall consumption is characterized by the behavior of *both* permanent- and current-income consumers. Leaving aside life-cycle income momentarily, aggregate consumption can be written compactly as

$$C = (\theta + p)[W + (1 - \lambda)H] + \lambda[Y - T]$$
$$= C^p + C^c. \qquad (36)$$

Agents with the ability to borrow choose their consumption (C^p) based on permanent income as before, which consists of financial wealth W and human wealth H.[91] Meanwhile, agents who face borrowing constraints have their consumption (C^c) constrained by current disposable income, where Y is labor income and T is lump-sum taxes. The parameter λ represents the proportion of households in the latter category, and total consumption is simply the sum of consumption by permanent-income and current-income consumers. In equation (36), λ can be interpreted as the degree of *excess sensitivity* of consumption to current disposable income compared with the case where every agent behaves according to the permanent-income hypothesis.

Returning to the life-cycle case, in the presence of age-dependent income (and taxes), as depicted in equation (21), aggregate consumption can be summarized as follows:

$$C = (\theta + p)[W + \beta(1 - \lambda_1)H_1 + (1 - \beta)(1 - \lambda_2)H_2]$$
$$+ (\beta\lambda_1 + (1 - \beta)\lambda_2)[Y - T]. \qquad (37)$$

With generation-specific income, the excess sensitivity of consumption to income now depends on the relative share of aggregate disposable income held by current-income consumers—described by the coefficient $\beta\lambda_1 + (1 - \beta)\lambda_2$—rather than on the

proportion of liquidity-constrained consumers in the population.[92]

Population and Productivity Growth

The basic model can also be further extended to the case of population and productivity growth (see also Buiter, 1988, and Weil, 1989). In the case of a growing population, the rate of population growth n is equal to the difference between the birth and death rates: $n = b - p$. The size of the total "population" at each moment in time is given by $N(t) = e^{nt}$, where $N(0)$ is normalized to unity. In the dynastic case, N would represent the number of dynastic families; if the number of members within these family were constant, then the total population would be proportional to the number of dynasties.[93]

Similarly, we can introduce long-run growth in productivity. Assuming (Harrod-neutral) labor-augmenting technical change, labor productivity is assumed to grow at a constant rate g. In other words, labor input L, measured in efficiency units, depends on both the number of workers and the efficiency of each worker: $L(t) = N(t)e^{gt}$. In the case where N represents the number of dynasties (rather than individuals), the labor force would be proportional to the number of these households. As with the population, the level of productivity at $t = 0$ is normalized to unity.

In the case of overlapping generations with life-cycle income, further substantive modifications are needed in the case of population growth. Specifically, to ensure adding up, individual labor income is now expressed as a function of aggregate labor income *per capita*:

$$y(s,t) = [a_1 e^{-\alpha_1(t-s)} + a_2 e^{-\alpha_2(t-s)}]Y(t)e^{-nt};$$
$$\frac{a_1 b}{\alpha_1 + b} + \frac{a_2 b}{\alpha_2 + b} = 1. \qquad (38)$$

The second part of this expression reflects the adding-up restriction on the parameters in terms of the *birth* (rather than death) rate, so that individual incomes sum to aggregate income over all generations; the earlier example in the text showed the simpler case where $b = p$ (that is, stationary population). The dynamic equations for human wealth (in labor

---

[91]From the equation, permanent-income consumers who comprise $1 - \lambda$ of the population hold all the financial wealth W in the economy. This is because agents are born without wealth and younger agents do not save (that is, accumulate wealth) initially while liquidity constrained.

[92]By adding up, we have $\beta \equiv a_1 p/(p + \alpha_1)$, $\lambda_1 \equiv 1 - e^{-(\alpha_1 + p)(t - \tau(t))}$, $\lambda_2 \equiv 1 - e^{-(\alpha_2 + p)(t - \iota(t))}$, where $\iota(t)$ is an index of the oldest generation still liquidity constrained at time t. By construction, $\lambda_2 > \lambda_1$, and both parameters can be greater than λ for plausible (hump-shaped) income profiles.

[93]In terms of specific cohorts, the number of individuals (or dynasties) born as part of cohort s is a proportion of the contemporaneous population given by $N(s,s) = bN(s)$, and the number of these individuals surviving at time $t \geq s$ is given by $N(s,t) = bN(s)e^{-p(t-s)}$.

Table 7. Extended Closed Economy Model with Liquidity Constraints and Population and Productivity Growth

$$c_t = (\theta + p)[w_t + \beta(1 - \lambda_1)h_{1t} + (1 - \beta)(1 - \lambda_2)h_{2t}]$$
$$+ (\beta\lambda_1 + (1 - \beta)\lambda_2)[y_t - \tau_t]$$

$$i_t = (q_t - 1 + \delta + n + g)k_{t-1}$$

$$\Delta k_t = f(k_t) - c_t - gv_t - a_t - (\delta + n + g)k_{t-1}$$

$$\Delta b_t = (r_t - n - g)b_{t-1} + gv_t - \tau_t$$

$$h_t = \beta h_{1t} + (1 - \beta)h_{2t}$$

$$\Delta h_{1t} = (r_t + p + \alpha_1 - g)h_1 - [y_t - \tau_t]$$

$$\Delta h_{2t} = (r_t + p + \alpha_2 - g)h_{2t-1} - [y_t - \tau_t]$$

efficiency units) under life-cycle income are derived analogously:[94]

$$h = \beta h_1 + (1 - \beta)h_2, \tag{39}$$

$$\dot{h}_1 = (r + p + \alpha_1 - g)h_1 - [y - \tau], \tag{40}$$

and

$$\dot{h}_2 = (r + p + \alpha_2 - g)h_2 - [y - \tau]. \tag{41}$$

For n and $\mu > 0$, we normalize aggregate variables (denoted by lowercase) in terms of labor measured in efficiency units.[95] Accordingly (normalized), consumption with life-cycle income and liquidity constraints would be modified as follows:

$$c = (\theta + p)[w + \beta(1 - \lambda_1)h_1 + (1 - \beta)(1 - \lambda_2)h_2]$$
$$+ (\beta\lambda_1 + (1 - \beta)\lambda_2)[y - \tau]. \tag{42}$$

Under the assumption of life-cycle behavior, the set of revised equations in discrete time in the closed economy model with population or productivity growth and liquidity constraints is summarized in Table 7.

Income Profiles: Theory and Calibration

To simulate the implications of life-cycle saving in the model, we must calibrate the degree of con-

cavity in age-earnings profiles. This subsection discusses some specification issues and then describes the data set, the estimated earnings profile, and the calibration that we adopt.

Specification Issues

To characterize the time profile of earnings, individual incomes are represented (following the previous discussion) as a time-varying, generation-specific weight $\omega(s,t)$ on income per capita for the economy as whole. Specifically, labor income $y(s,t)$ for a member of generation s at time t ($\geq s$), as a proportion of average income per capita, can be written as

$$y(s,t) = \left[a_1 e^{-\alpha_1(t-s)} + a_2 e^{-\alpha_2(t-s)}\right]\frac{Y(t)}{N(t)}, \tag{43}$$

where Y is aggregate labor income, and N is the size of the population. Several characteristics of the earnings profiles and parameter restrictions with respect to equation (43) are worth noting:

- *Nonmonotonicity.* To guarantee that income profiles do not rise or fall monotonically, we require that a_1 and a_2 be of opposite sign. Without loss of generality, we further specify $a_1 > 0$ and $a_2 < 0$. To ensure concavity, two additional restrictions are needed:

  Initially increasing. For incomes to rise initially, the time derivative of $\omega(s,t)$ at $s = t$ must be strictly positive, requiring $\alpha_1 a_1 < -\alpha_2 a_2$.

  Eventually declining. To also ensure that labor earnings eventually fall off with retirement, a sufficient condition has $\alpha_1, \alpha_2 > 0$, which in combination with the previous assumptions will generate a hump-shaped time profile for labor income.

- *Nonnegativity.* For individual incomes to always remain positive given aggregate income (that is, for $\omega(s,t) \geq 0$ for all t), a necessary condition has $a_1 \geq -a_2$, which is also sufficient provided that we also have $\alpha_2 > \alpha_1$.[96]

- *Adding up.* Integrating over all generations, individual labor incomes must add up to aggregate labor income, requiring that

  $$\frac{a_1 b}{\alpha_1 + b} + \frac{a_2 b}{\alpha_2 + b} = 1, \text{ where } b \text{ is the birth rate.}$$

In light of the parameter restrictions on the two exponential terms, the weighting function can be thought of as the sum of two opposing factors:

---

[94]We now have $\beta \equiv a_1 b/(b + \alpha_1)$, $\lambda_1 \equiv 1 - e^{-(\alpha_1 + b)(t - \iota(t))}$, $\lambda_2 \equiv 1 - e^{-(\alpha_2 + b)(t - \iota(t))}$.

[95]Lowercase variables with a time and a generation index refer to individual measures, whereas lowercase variables with only a time argument reflect per capita measures (in units of labor efficiency): $x(t) \equiv X(t)/L(t) = X(t)e^{-(n+g)t}$. Government spending in labor efficiency units is denoted gv_t to avoid confusion with the growth rate.

[96]Together, the conditions for nonnegative and initially increasing income profiles imply

$$\alpha_2 a_1 > -\alpha_2 a_2 > \alpha_1 a_1 > -\alpha_1 a_2.$$

(1) declining labor supply (gradual retirement),[97] which by itself reduces labor income over time, and (2) the declining costs of inexperience (wage gains from seniority), which increases labor income over time. In combination, the effects of experience and seniority cause incomes to rise early on, but the effects of (gradual) retirement eventually dominate to lower wage earnings. Together, these "structural" factors can be thought of as underlying the concave earnings profile over an agent's lifetime.

The simple two-exponential specification can also be generalized to allow for a broader range of time profiles for labor income. Specifically, we can expand (43) as follows:

$$y(s,t) = \left[\sum_{i=1}^{k} a_i e^{-\alpha_i(t-s)}\right] \frac{Y(t)}{N(t)}, \tag{44}$$

for some integer k. This more general specification is used later in the estimation along with the corresponding parameter restrictions on the a_i and α_i terms to ensure adding up and concavity.

Data and Estimation

Using statistics on labor income and employment by age for the United States, a data set was constructed containing the cross-sectional distribution of real labor income at selected ages during each year from 1980 to 1995.[98] The ages used were 20, 30, 40, 50, 60, and 75 years, essentially representing the midpoint (or median) ages for each of six cohort ranges.[99] This provided 16 years of data on the cross-sectional distribution of labor income for each of six age groups, for a total of 96 observations.

To characterize the time profile of labor earnings empirically, we estimate a structural time-series representation of these cross-sectional income distributions. Specifically, we assume that a typical individual's earnings over his or her lifetime follow the time pattern suggested by the average income profile seen in the cross-sectional distribution. The information in the cross-sectional profile is then used to estimate a time-series relationship between labor earnings and age, capturing the life-cycle pattern of an individual's labor income.

In equations (43) and (44), labor income is expressed in absolute terms (that is, in consumption units). However, we can obtain a measure of *relative* income by expressing individual labor income for a particular cohort as a proportion of income per capita for the aggregate economy:

$$ry(s,t) \equiv y(s,t)N(t)/Y(t) = \sum_{i=1}^{k} a_i e^{\alpha_i(t-s)}. \tag{45}$$

Relative income profiles have the advantage of isolating the parameters of interest and are more likely to reflect the institutional aspects of labor markets (for example, seniority wages, age of retirement, and so on) that interest us. The shapes of the relative income profiles are also likely to be more stable (and thus comparable) over time than absolute income profiles, given time-variation in aggregate labor productivity.[100]

To estimate the shape of the earnings profile, we employ a nonlinear least squares (NLLS) estimation of equation (45) using our data on relative income distributions.[101] However, the specification based on the sum of two (or more) exponential terms has a multiplicity of possible parameterizations (that is, local maxima). Consequently, we make certain identifying restrictions by imposing values for the birth rate b or a given set of coefficients a_1, a_2, and so on, to obtain conditional estimates of the parameters of interest (that is, α's).[102] This narrows the parameter search considerably and provides more robust estimates for alternative starting values for the estimated parameters. Conditional NLLS estimates of equation (45) are shown in Table 8 for one case with $k = 2$ and for two cases with $k = 3$.

The estimates in Table 8 do reasonably well in fitting the cross-sectional income distributions for the United States and are generally sensible. The plots of the fitted income profiles based on each set of estimates are shown in Figure 3. The specifications with an added exponential term ($k = 3$) have somewhat better fits, although the specification with the highest R^2 (that is, in column 2) yields an implausibly high birth rate (6 percent) and eventually turns negative. For these reasons, and others discussed below, the estimates in column 3 of Table 8 are preferred.

Steady-State Calibration

To ascertain whether the model's calibration of birth rates and death rates is sensible, several aspects

---

[97]In reality, individuals generally experience a discontinuous fall in labor supply and wage earnings with retirement. However, given that individuals retire at different ages, the representative income profile averaged over many individuals may be approximated with a smooth function. See also Blanchard (1985) and Saint-Paul (1992).

[98]Cross-sectional data on real labor income were readily available only for Canada and the United States. For convenience, only the U.S. data are used, although both data sets appear somewhat similar.

[99]The cohort ranges are 18–24, 25–34, 35–44, 45–54, 55–64, and 65 +.

[100]This will certainly be the case if aggregate labor productivity growth affects absolute labor incomes for all age groups proportionately without affecting the relative (cross-sectional) distribution of income.

[101]NLLS estimates of the vector of parameters (α, a) seek to minimize the sum of squared residuals u from the following regression: $ry_t = f(t, \alpha, a) + u_t$, where $f(.)$ follows from equation (46).

[102]The imposed parameters are obtained through grid search.

Table 8. Relative Income Profiles: Nonlinear Least Squares Estimates

Parameters	(1) $k = 2$	(2) $k = 3$	(3) $k = 3$
α_1	0.051**	0.010**	0.078**
α_2	0.061	0.019**	0.121**
α_3	...	−0.004	0.091
a_1	20.00	40.00	100.00
a_2	−19.56	−30.00	40.00
a_3	...	−9.56	−139.56
b	0.031**	0.057**	0.03
$\bar{R}^2$	0.78	0.98	0.88
DW	1.95	2.49	1.72

Note: ** indicates significance at the 5 percent level; entries in italics denote parameter values that were imposed (or redundant) in the conditional estimates. The first $k - 1$ exponents (α's) are estimated directly, and the kth term is determined from the adding-up restriction.

Model: $ry_t = \sum_{i=1}^{k} a_i e^{-\alpha_i(t-20)}$

Restrictions: $\sum_{i=1}^{k} \dfrac{a_i b}{\alpha_i + b} = 1$; $\sum_{i=1}^{k} a_i = \bar{ry}_{20}$.

Figure 3. Estimated Income Profiles

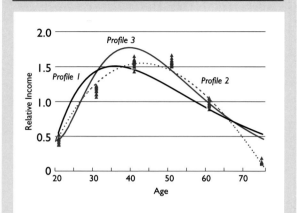

Note: Triangles represent historical data points on the age-earnings distribution, centered at the ages of 20, 30, 40, 50, 60, and 75. The three labor income profiles, which reflect the parameter estimates reported in the corresponding columns of Table 8, depict the per capita incomes for each age cohort relative to average income per capita across all age groups.

need to be considered. First, as the death rate is directly related to the length of an individual's planning horizon in the model, it should broadly reflect measures of life expectancy. Second, the difference between birth and death rates in the model represents the rate of population growth of working-age individuals and retirees, which also guides the choice of these rates. In long-run steady state, to obtain a stationary population, the model further requires *equal* birth and death rates at their long-run (replacement) levels. At those levels, the model's implications for the steady-state age distribution offer yet another guide as to the choice of these magnitudes.

In the presence of a stationary population, the model and its constant death rate assumption can generate steady-state age distributions that broadly mimic those implied by demographic projections. For example, to match an elderly dependency ratio of 44 percent, defined as the population 65 years and older as a share of the working-age population (ages 20–64), the model requires a long-run birth and death rate of about 2½ percent. However, the model's simple assumption that the (conditional) probability of death is identical at all ages implies a

steady-state age distribution that tends to overstate the number of individuals in younger age groups and understate the number of middle-age and older individuals,[103] as illustrated in Table 9.[104]

Specifying death rates of 2–2½ percent suggests individual planning horizons of about 40–50 years, or life expectancy (at age 20, when individuals are "born" into the youngest cohort of workers) of about 60–70 years. Away from steady state, the 3 percent birth rates in Table 8 are quite plausible and, given these death rates, imply a growth rate for the (adult) population of about ½ of 1 percent to 1 percent, consistent with the historical figures for the United States during the sample period.[105]

---

[103]The theoretical distribution also includes an asymptotic tail of (arbitrarily) old people, whereas in reality this distribution is clearly truncated at some finite maximum age. This latter issue is not too severe a problem given that the very old generations form an increasingly small (infinitesimal) proportion of the population.

[104]As a share of the total population, the number of survivors from a generation born at time s remaining at time t is equal to $be^{-p(t-s)}$; with a stationary population in steady state, $b = p$ and $n = 0$. Using this expression, we approximate the model's steady-state age distribution across the (discrete) age groups as shown in the table.

[105]The calculated birth rate—defined as the relative size of new arrivals (that is, youngest cohort) as a share of the existing adult population—varied from 2½ percent to 3 percent for the United States over the sample period. The average growth rate for the adult population was about ½ of 1 percent over the same period, implying a death rate of 2–2½ percent.

Table 9. Theoretical and Projected Steady-State Age Distributions
(In percent of adult population)

	Age Group						Dependency Ratio
	20–24	25–34	35–44	45–54	55–64	65+	
Steady-state model	11.9	19.8	15.4	12.0	9.3	31.6	46
World Bank projections[1]	7.8	15.6	15.5	15.4	15.1	30.6	44

[1]For the United States, based on Bos and others (1994).

Estimates of the Mark III Consumption Function

The previous subsection provides a calibration of the parameters (for example, α_1, α_2) underlying the life-cycle component of the consumption function in Mark III. To complete the calibration of the consumption-saving model, we also require an estimate of the sensitivity parameter λ, representing the share of consumption accounted for by income-constrained individuals, and the intertemporal elasticity of substitution σ^{-1} in consumption, which need not equal unity (that is, log utility case) as assumed (for convenience) in Tables 5 through 7.

Table 10 presents a summary of the system of equations that make up the consumption-saving model in Mark III. The parameters associated with the life-cycle profile of labor income (that is, a_i, α_i, b) are taken from column 3 of Table 8. Estimates of the sensitivity of consumption to disposable income λ and the intertemporal elasticity of substitution σ^{-1} are also shown.

The estimates in Table 10, based on annual data for 1982–96, reflect, for the seven major industrial countries, pooled estimates of the intertemporal elasticity of substitution (σ^{-1}) and country-specific estimates of the share of income-constrained consumption. The model is estimated with instrumental variables, using as instruments $C(t-1)$, $C_{DI}(t-1)$, $WH1(t-1)$, $WH2(t-1)$, and $WH3(t-1)$. The estimated magnitude of the elasticity of substitution is highly significant and broadly consistent with the magnitudes of estimates from other sources.[106] Box

---

[106]The estimate of 0.41 here relates to the proportion of consumption that is interest sensitive and needs to be multiplied by a factor of $(1 - \lambda)$ before comparison with estimates of the elasticity of substitution for aggregate consumption. Patterson and Pesaran (1992) and Attanasio and Weber (1993) place the latter in the range of 0.1 to 0.3; Hall (1988) argues that it may be lower than 0.2.

Table 10. Estimated Parameters of the Mark III Consumption-Saving Model

Aggregate-consumption: $C = C_{DI} + C_{PI}$

Income-constrained consumption:
$$C_{DI} = YD[\lambda_1\beta_1 + \lambda_2\beta_2 + \lambda_3(1 - \beta_1 - \beta_2)]$$

Wealth-constrained consumption:
$$C_{PI} = MPC(WK + M/P + B/P + NFA/P + WH)$$

Inverse of marginal propensity to consume:
$$MPC_{t+1}^{-1} = \{1 - \sigma^{-1}[(1 - \sigma)(rsr_t + p_t) - (\tau_t + p_t)]\}MPC_t^{-1} - 1$$

Human wealth:
$$WH = \beta_1(1 - \lambda_1)WH1 + \beta_2(1 - \lambda_2)WH2 + (1 - \beta_1 - \beta_2)(1 - \lambda_3)WH3$$

i^{th} component of human wealth:
$$WH(i)_{t+1} = WH(i)_t(1 + rsr_t + p_t) - YD_t$$

$$\lambda_i = 1 - \exp\{[(\alpha_i + b)/b]\log(1 - \lambda)\}; \quad \beta_i = \frac{a_ib}{\alpha_i + b}$$

	σ^{-1}	λ	R^2	SE
Canada	0.41** (0.017)	0.75** (0.09)	0.971	0.022
France	0.41** (0.017)	0.49** (0.01)	0.988	0.010
Germany	0.41** (0.017)	0.46** (0.01)	0.982	0.019
Italy	0.41** (0.017)	0.50** (0.02)	0.874	0.033
Japan	0.41** (0.017)	0.28** (0.01)	0.974	0.026
United Kingdom	0.41** (0.017)	0.46** (0.01)	0.936	0.034
United States	0.41** (0.017)	0.30** (0.09)	0.993	0.015

Note: Standard errors reported in parentheses; ** indicates that estimated coefficient is significantly different from zero at the 5 percent significance level.

Box 9. The Global Crowding-Out Effects of Government Debt

As in most modern macro models, the extent of fiscal crowding out in response to a government debt shock depends critically on (1) the degree to which consumers are assumed to count government bonds as net wealth, (2) the relationship assumed between aggregate consumption and disposable income, and (3) the assumed sensitivity of aggregate consumption to changes in interest rates. If consumers are connected to all future generations by operative intergenerational transfers, increases in government debt will not crowd out private investment because consumers will change their saving rate today to prepare for tax liabilities in the future. This is referred to as the Ricardian equivalence hypothesis because taxes today (that is, tax financing of government spending) are equivalent to taxes in the future (that is, deficit financing of government spending). For reasons discussed in the main text, MULTIMOD does not adopt the Ricardian equivalence hypothesis, but rather reflects the view that households adjust their saving by only part of the higher future tax burden associated with higher levels of government debt. In effect, agents treat a portion of their holdings of government bonds as net wealth because they "excessively" discount the higher tax liabilities in the future required to service the government's interest payments on its debt.

Two explanations why full Ricardian equivalence does not apply in practice are embodied in the properties of Mark III. First, because a significant fraction of consumers cannot borrow against their future labor in-

come, their expenditure is effectively constrained by their current disposable income. Second, consumers who are constrained by wealth rather than by disposable income are assumed not to internalize the tax burden that will be passed on to future generations. Thus, wealth-constrained consumers are assumed to incompletely adjust their saving rates in response to higher future tax liabilities because they realize that future generations will partly share the tax burden associated with higher levels of government debt. Both imperfect capital markets and the disconnectedness of today's generation from future generations imply that higher levels of government debt will be associated with a tendency to overconsume available resources. This tendency to overconsume will result in higher real interest rates and eventually in a lower capital stock and lower sustainable levels of real income and consumption.

The increase in interest rates required to eliminate the tendency to overconsume available resources will depend critically on the interest sensitivity of consumption. If consumption were highly sensitive to changes in real interest rates, then only a small rise in interest rates would be required to induce consumers to adjust their saving rates in response to an increase in government debt. However, the empirical literature, including Mark III estimates, suggests that the interest sensitivity of consumption and saving is low. Thus, this evidence also suggests significant long-run crowding-out effects of government debt.

9, which focuses on the crowding-out effects of government debt, provides some perspective on the sensitivity of these fiscal effects to certain critical assumptions and parameter estimates.

Appendix. Fiscal Policy Effects in a Small Open Economy

Two experiments are considered here to illustrate the dynamic effects of fiscal policy in a small open economy. The simulations use the Canada bloc of MULTIMOD to explore the effects of (1) a permanent increase in government debt that is a result of a temporary tax cut, holding constant the level of real government spending, and (2) a permanent increase in real government spending, holding tax rates constant temporarily before raising them to subsequently stabilize the ratio of government debt to GDP. In both shocks, tax rates are adjusted after the fifth year to raise the debt-to-GDP ratio to a level that is 10 percentage points higher than in the baseline. In each case, the current reduction in public saving (that is, deficit financing) and its consequences for future tax burdens have important

macroeconomic effects as private agents are unable, or fail, to fully internalize the implications of the government's intertemporal budget constraint. When consumers "excessively discount" future tax liabilities or are "excessively sensitive" to current disposable income, changes in fiscal policy can have relatively large effects on the real economy, reflecting significant departures from Ricardian equivalence. (See Box 9 for further discussion of the factors underpinning the Ricardian equivalence hypothesis.)

Higher Public Debt Through a Temporary Tax Cut

Figure 4 shows the effects of a temporary five-year tax cut, holding government spending constant, that leads to a permanent increase of 10 percentage points in the ratio of government debt to GDP.[107] Higher public borrowing is accompanied by a pickup in economic activity in the near term, as both

---

[107]The tax cut takes the form of a lowering of the basic tax rate by 2 percentage points of nominal GDP for five years, holding constant the tax rate on capital income; it thus amounts essentially to a lowering of the tax rate on labor income.

Steady-State Effects of Simultaneous 10 Percentage Point Increases in Ratios of Government Debt to GDP of All Industrial Countries

	Without an Increase in Distortionary Taxes on Capital	With an Increase in Distortionary Taxes on Capital
Output (in percent)	−1.1	−1.6
Consumption (in percent)	−1.0	−1.4
Capital stock (in percent)	−3.4	−4.7
Real interest rate (basis points)	31.0	32.0

The table provides some estimates of the long-run crowding-out effects of simultaneous 10 percentage point increases in ratios of government debt to GDP of all industrial countries. The table includes estimates of the long-run effects on real interest rates, aggregate output, consumption, and the capital stock for all industrial countries. Two cases are shown, representing different assumptions regarding which taxes are raised to meet the higher steady-state interest obligations on government debt. In the first case, the basic tax rate on nominal GDP is raised, holding constant the tax rate on capital, so that the increase in taxes is essentially borne by labor. Unlike capital taxes, labor taxes are nondistortionary in Mark III because the labor supply is assumed to be exogenous in the long run. In the second case, we allow the tax rate on capital income to rise by the same amount as the basic tax rate on GDP.

In the first case, the real interest rate rises by 31 basis points, and the capital stock declines by 3.4 percent. This reduces potential output by 1.1 percent, and the sustainable level of consumption declines by 1.0 percent. When distortionary capital taxes are assumed to partially finance the increase in the debt-service burden, there are slightly larger crowding-out effects on output, consumption, and the capital stock.

private consumption and saving rise with the fall in taxes and the increase in disposable income. An increase in the fiscal deficit thus places upward pressure on interest rates and the exchange rate initially, leading to some crowding out of investment and net exports. Because the increase in public dissaving is not fully offset by a rise in private saving, the current account deficit tends to widen, and the greater reliance on foreign saving leads to an increase in net external debt.

In the long run, private consumption and disposable income are lower, reflecting the higher taxes required to finance higher interest payments on higher public debt. The long-run levels of investment, the capital stock, and output decline very slightly in association with the higher level of debt because the steady-state real interest rate in the individual country models is assumed to be tied down to the (exogenous) world real interest rate.[108] Meanwhile, net ex-

ports rise in the steady state—in association with a permanent decline in the real competitiveness index—to finance the higher interest payments to foreigners resulting from higher external debt.

Higher Public Debt with Permanently Higher Government Spending

Figure 5 shows the effects of a permanent 2 percentage point increase in the ratio of government spending to GDP, holding tax rates constant for five years and subsequently adjusting the basic tax rate to stabilize the ratio of public debt to GDP at a level that is 10 percentage points higher than in the baseline. This shock also leads to increases in output, interest rates, and the exchange rate in the short term. Higher interest rates and an appreciated currency tend to lower investment and net exports in the near term, and the fall in national (private plus public) saving tends to worsen the current account balance and increase the level of net foreign liabilities.

In the long run, private consumption and disposable income are again lower because of higher taxes. However, the long-run decline in disposable

---

[108]In the full model simulations, the world real interest rate is endogenous and determined by equilibrating world savings and investment. Bayoumi and Laxton (1994) consider the effects of fiscal policy when real interest rate differentials depend on the level of government debt.

Figure 4. Higher Public Debt Through a Temporary Tax Cut in Canada
(Deviations from baseline values, in percent)

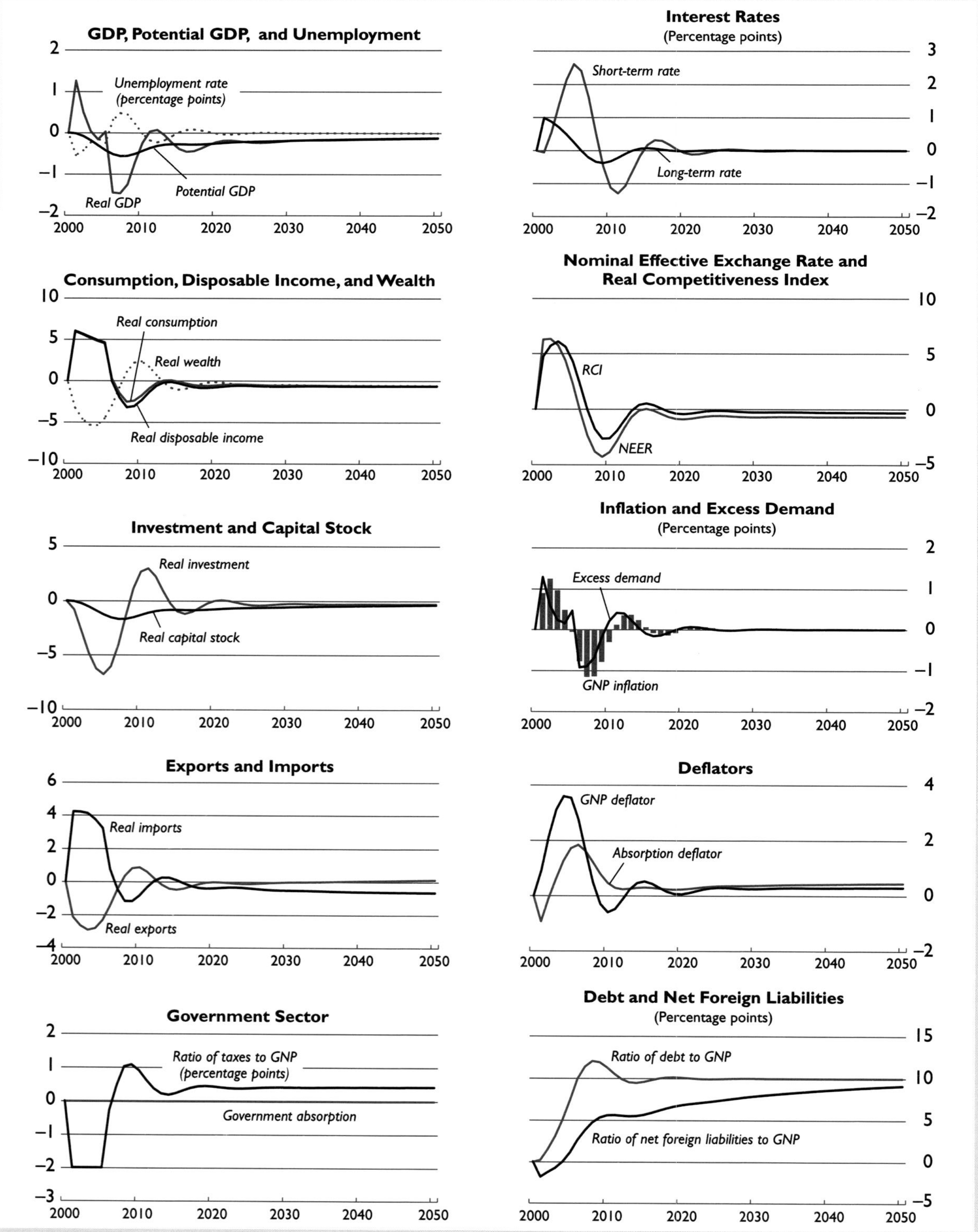

GDP, Potential GDP, and Unemployment

Unemployment rate (percentage points)

Real GDP

Potential GDP

Consumption, Disposable Income, and Wealth

Real consumption

Real wealth

Real disposable income

Investment and Capital Stock

Real investment

Real capital stock

Exports and Imports

Real imports

Real exports

Government Sector

Ratio of taxes to GNP (percentage points)

Government absorption

Interest Rates
(Percentage points)

Short-term rate

Long-term rate

Nominal Effective Exchange Rate and Real Competitiveness Index

RCI

NEER

Inflation and Excess Demand
(Percentage points)

Excess demand

GNP inflation

Deflators

GNP deflator

Absorption deflator

Debt and Net Foreign Liabilities
(Percentage points)

Ratio of debt to GNP

Ratio of net foreign liabilities to GNP

Figure 5. Higher Public Debt with Permanently Higher Fiscal Spending in Canada
(Deviations from baseline values, in percent)

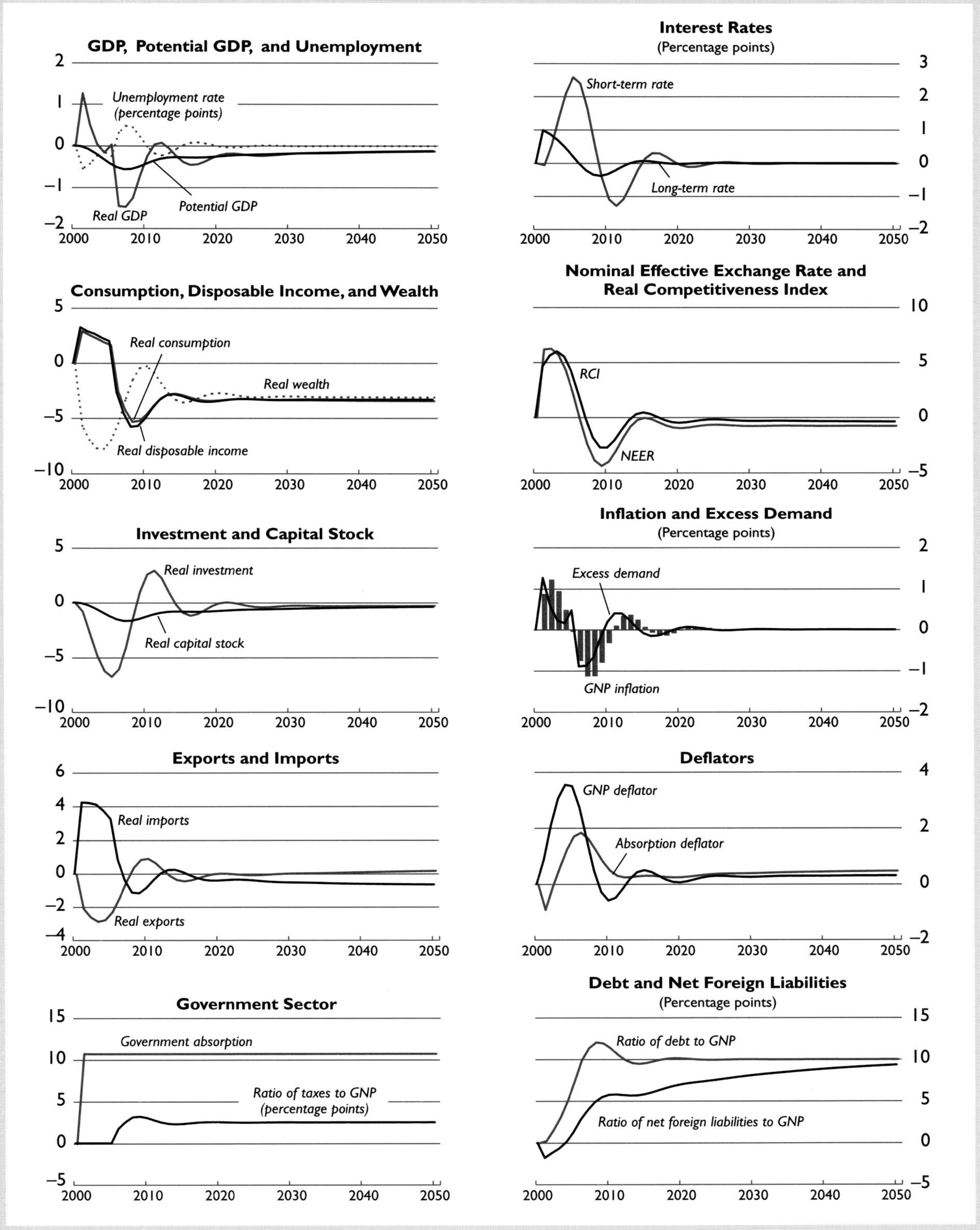

GDP, Potential GDP, and Unemployment
Unemployment rate (percentage points)
Real GDP
Potential GDP
2
1
0
–1
–2
2000
2010
2020
2030
2040
2050
Interest Rates
(Percentage points)
Short-term rate
Long-term rate
3
2
1
0
–1
–2
Consumption, Disposable Income, and Wealth
Real consumption
Real wealth
Real disposable income
5
0
–5
–10
Nominal Effective Exchange Rate and Real Competitiveness Index
RCI
NEER
10
5
0
–5
Investment and Capital Stock
Real investment
Real capital stock
5
0
–5
–10
Inflation and Excess Demand
(Percentage points)
Excess demand
GNP inflation
2
1
0
–1
–2
Exports and Imports
Real imports
Real exports
6
4
2
0
–2
–4
Deflators
GNP deflator
Absorption deflator
4
2
0
–2
Government Sector
Government absorption
Ratio of taxes to GNP (percentage points)
15
10
5
0
–5
Debt and Net Foreign Liabilities
(Percentage points)
Ratio of debt to GNP
Ratio of net foreign liabilities to GNP
15
10
5
0
–5

income is somewhat larger for the government expenditure shock, which induces a larger crowding-out effect on private consumption to accommodate higher public consumption. But as was the case for the temporary tax cut, the real interest rate converges back to the world rate of interest as output, investment, and the capital stock return to their baseline levels. Meanwhile, on the external side, a steady-state real depreciation is again required to boost net exports and finance the larger stock of net external debt.

The short-run effects of government expenditure and tax rate shocks are strikingly similar for Canada because the proportion of consumers who base their consumption on disposable income is estimated to be large. For the other major industrial countries, short-run government spending multipliers tend to be significantly greater than the tax multipliers.

VI Investment

Simulations of the macroeconomic effects of various policy measures or other exogenous shocks depend importantly on how one models the responsiveness of the components of aggregate demand to changes in interest rates and exchange rates. In this regard, finding a realistic specification for the behavior of investment—one of the most volatile components of aggregate demand—is a key challenge in macroeconometric modeling. Unfortunately, the effort to characterize aggregate investment behavior has not been a highly successful endeavor in empirical economics.

This section describes the dynamics of investment behavior and capital accumulation in MULTIMOD Mark III, along with the production structure of the model. As in MULTIMOD Mark II, the Mark III model of capital and investment dynamics is based on the q theory of Tobin (1969). The major changes from the Mark II version include the integration of the q theory with the cost-of-adjustment model of Lucas (1967) and Treadway (1969), as well as a significant simplification in the treatment of historical costs, tax credits, and other details (see Meredith, 1991).

In the Mark III setup, firms maximize the expected net present value of future earnings subject to technological constraints. Let $\prod(K_{s-1})$ denote the revenue function of a representative firm, A_s adjustment costs, and I_s gross investment, all in period s. The representative firm is assumed to have the objective of maximizing the expected discounted sum of its future profits, defined as

$$E_t = \left[\sum_{s=t}^{\infty} \rho^{t-s} \prod(K_{s-1}) - A_s - I_s \right], \tag{46}$$

where ρ denotes the firm's discount factor. The revenue function is based on the following Cobb-Douglas production function:

$$Y_t = \zeta_t K_{t-1}^{\beta} L_t^{1-\beta}, \tag{47}$$

where Y_t is GDP, β is the share of capital, and ζ_t measures the level of total factor productivity.[109]

Following the tradition in the investment literature, adjustment costs are specified in terms of squared deviations from the steady-state level of the investment-to-capital ratio. The steady-state value of this ratio is determined by the sum of the depreciation rate (δ) and the growth rate of the real economy (g).[110] The exact specification used for adjustment costs is

$$A_t = \frac{\chi}{2} \left[\frac{I_t}{K_{t-1}} - (\delta + g) \right]^2 K_{t-1}, \tag{48}$$

where K_{t-1} is the capital stock at the beginning of period t, and χ is a parameter that measures the size of the adjustment costs.

The firm maximizes the expected net present value of future profits with respect to capital and investment in equation (46), subject to the technical law of motion for the capital stock:

$$K_t = I_t + (1 - \delta) K_{t-1}. \tag{49}$$

The first-order condition with respect to investment determines optimal investment as a function of Tobin's q:

$$I_t = \left(\delta + g + \frac{q_t - 1}{\chi} \right) K_{t-1}, \tag{50}$$

where q_t is the shadow price of capital, or the ratio of the market value of a marginal unit of capital to its replacement cost.[111] According to this relationship, it will be profitable to increase the investment-to-capital ratio above its steady-state level as long as q_t is greater than one. Conversely, if q_t is less than one, the investment ratio will fall below its steady-state level. Equation (50) can be rewritten as follows:

$$q_t = \chi \left[\frac{I_t}{K_{t-1}} - (\delta + g) \right] + 1. \tag{51}$$

The first-order condition with respect to the capital stock determines the law of motion for Tobin's q:

---

[109]It is assumed that the revenue function has already been maximized vis-à-vis other variable production factors.

[110]The growth rate of GDP is a composite variable comprising technological progress and labor force dynamics.

[111]Technically, q_t is the Lagrange multiplier on the constraint in equation (49).

$$q_t = (1-\delta)E_t\,\rho_{t+1}q_{t+1} + E_t\rho_{t+1}\left[\frac{\partial\Pi_{t+1}}{\partial K_t} - \frac{\partial A_{t+1}}{\partial K_t}\right]. \quad (52)$$

This equation indicates that q_t, the market value of the firm for each unit of capital at time t, is determined by the expected discounted value of q in period $t+1$, corrected for depreciation, plus the difference between the expected discounted marginal product of capital and the marginal cost of adding new capacity in period $t+1$.

The importance of adjustment costs for the evolution of the market value of capital is best seen by differentiating equation (48) to obtain the derivative of adjustment costs with respect to capital:

$$\frac{\partial A_t}{\partial K_{t-1}} = \frac{\chi}{2}\left[\frac{I_t}{K_{t-1}} - (\delta + g)\right]^2$$

$$- \chi\frac{I_t}{K_{t-1}}\left[\frac{I_t}{K_{t-1}} - (\delta + g)\right]. \quad (53)$$

When χ equals zero, adjustment costs are zero as well, and this term drops out of the law of motion for Tobin's q. In that case, it can be seen from equation (51) that q always equals one and that at any point in time the value of the capital stock equals its replacement cost. This is so because it only makes sense to have less than full adjustment of the capital stock when adjustment is costly. If there are no adjustment costs, it is optimal to keep the capital stock at its equilibrium level in every period.[112]

In steady state, the above framework simplifies substantially. With the capital stock growing in line with GDP, gross investment as a percent of the capital stock equals the sum of the economy's growth rate and the depreciation rate. In that case, Tobin's q equals one and the real value of the capital stock equals its replacement cost. According to equation (48), moreover, adjustment costs are zero, reflecting the tradition of characterizing such costs as a quadratic function of the deviation of the investment-capital ratio from its steady-state value.

To implement this setup, a set of simplifying assumptions are needed. Defining the real market value of the capital stock as

$$WK_t = q_t K_{t-1}, \quad (55)$$

we use the following expression, based on an approximation to equation (52), for the law of motion of the real value of the capital stock in the numerical model:

$$WK_{t+1} = WK_t\,[1 + r_t + \delta_t + rprem_t + (K_t/K_{t-1} - 1)]$$

$$- \left[(1-\tau)\beta Y_t - \frac{\partial A_t}{\partial K_{t-1}}K_{t-1}\right]. \quad (56)$$

This equation indicates that the real value of the capital stock at time t equals the discounted expected value of next period's capital stock plus the discounted after-tax income accruing to capital after netting out the real resources taken up to adjust the capital stock. The discount factor used incorporates the real short-term interest rate (r_t) plus the rate of depreciation, the yield premium on capital ($rprem_t$), and the growth rate of the capital stock. The yield premium, which is treated as a residual in the simulations, reflects the difference between the marginal product of capital and the real interest rate; τ is the tax rate on capital income.

Conceptually, the presence of the yield premium reflects a decision to use the marginal product of capital, rather than the "risk-free" real interest rate, to discount future market values of the capital stock. This is done to ensure that in steady state the replacement cost of the capital stock equals its market value and, hence, that q equals unity.[113]

Although equations (51) and (52) and their steady-state counterparts provide a fully determined model of the dynamic and steady-state behavior of investment, some important considerations are missing. Despite the theoretical appeal of the link between investment and Tobin's q, the particular form of the relationship described by equations (50) and (51) is only partially, if at all, reflected in historical data. One limitation of the model is that it does not take account of the irreversibility of investment—and the option value of waiting to invest—as analyzed in Bertola (1988), Bertola and Caballero (1990), and Dixit and Pindyck (1994). In addition, the theoretical framework ignores time-to-build features and the as-

---

[112]This model is a special case of a more general investment function that includes imperfectly competitive goods markets and imperfect capital markets. Substituting equations (51), (53), and the first derivative of (47) into equation (52) gives an equation that can be estimated in the following "flexible-accelerator" form:

$$\frac{I_t}{K_{t-1}} = \kappa_0 + \kappa_1\frac{I_{t-1}}{K_{t-2}} + \kappa_2\left(\frac{I_{t-1}}{K_{t-2}}\right)^2 + \kappa_3\frac{Y_t}{K_{t-1}} + \kappa_4 r_{t-1} + \nu_t, \quad (54)$$

where the parameters κ are functions of the rate of depreciation, the growth rate of the economy, the tax rate on capital income, and the value of χ in the adjustment-cost function. While the presence of the quadratic term in equation (54) indicates the presence of adjustment costs, the absence of an aggregate cash-flow measure and the aggregate business sector debt implies that there are no distortions (tax-induced or other) that would lead to meaningful financial policies (that is, preference for equity over debt finance, or paying dividends). See Bond and Meghir (1994) for an in-depth discussion and empirical implementation and Epstein and Denny (1983) for a rigorous analysis of the flexible-accelerator specification of the adjustment-cost model.

[113]To maintain the consistency of the national income accounts in MULTIMOD, the marginal product of capital is also used in evaluating household wealth. In particular, since the marginal product of capital is larger than the real interest rate and is used to calculate the share of capital income in total income, it needs to be incorporated in the wealth terms used in consumption behavior as described in Section V, to make sure that aggregate factor income is consistent with the value of production.

sociated impact of planning horizons on actual investment figures. These considerations suggest that the contemporaneous relationship described in equation (50) is unrealistic and that changes in q may have lagged effects on investment. This motivates us to estimate the following variant of equation (50):

$$\frac{I_t}{K_{t-1}} - \delta - g = k_1 q_t + k_2 q_{t-1} + \varepsilon_t. \tag{57}$$

Equation (57) is estimated for a panel of 17 industrial countries based on annual data for 1975–96. This requires the construction of synthetic data for q and WK, which is done in two steps. In the first step, a value of 12 for χ is used to calculate q and WK based on equations (51) and (55).[114] As a second step, intended to obtain time series that are more consistent with the full model and to attenuate the endogeneity problem stemming from the fact that q is a forward-looking variable, the first-stage measures of q are regressed on the following instruments lagged one period: the log of GDP, the log of the capital stock, the log of real money balances, and the nominal interest rate. The fitted values from the instrumental variables regressions are then used in the estimation of (57).

Equation (58) reports the coefficients for this regression. Investment reacts positively to increases in q and its lag, with lagged q having a slightly larger impact:

$$\frac{I_t}{K_{t-1}} - \delta - g = 0.033 \, q_t + 0.048 \, q_{t-1}. \tag{58}$$
$$\qquad\qquad (32.92) \quad (54.06)$$

Some implications of this specification for the co-movements of investment, output, and real interest rates are illustrated in the appendix.

Appendix. Investment, Output, and Interest Rate Responses to Demand and Supply Shocks

It has proved difficult in small samples to find stable reduced-form equations for investment that depend on output and real interest rates, in part because the co-movements of these three variables are sensitive to the nature of the underlying shocks. To illus-

trate the potential problems with reduced-form models of investment, the U.K. bloc of MULTIMOD is used to simulate the effects of demand and supply shocks. This terminology is somewhat misleading because most shocks perturb both demand and supply; here, we simply follow the literature and define supply shocks to be shocks that have permanent effects on real variables, while demand shocks are those shocks that have only temporary, but often persistent, effects on real variables.

A Demand Shock Induced by Monetary Policy

The left column of Figure 6 shows the impulse responses of investment, real GDP, and the real short-term interest rate following a permanent 10 percent increase in the target money supply. Because prices are sticky in MULTIMOD, an increase in the target money supply results in a reduction in the short-term real interest rate. In the short run, investment and real GDP rise in response to the easing in monetary conditions. However, in the long run, prices adjust one for one with the increase in the money supply, and all three variables shown here return to their baseline paths.

A Demand Shock Induced by Fiscal Policy

The middle column of Figure 6 shows the impulse responses of investment, real GDP, and the real short-term interest rate following a temporary increase in government expenditures of 1 percent of baseline GDP. In the short run, there is a tendency for the real short-term interest rate to rise, which results in some crowding out of investment expenditures.[115] However, because the shock is short lived, real GDP and investment return to their baseline paths in the long run.

A Supply Shock

The right column of Figure 6 shows the impulse responses of investment, real GDP, and the real short-term interest rate following a permanent 1 percent increase in total factor productivity. In MULTIMOD, an increase in total factor productivity results in an increase in the desired capital stock; the investment-to-GDP ratio must rise above its new steady-state level in the short run in order to achieve this higher level of capital. In the short run, investment, GDP, and the real interest rate will tend to rise. In the long run, GDP and investment are higher and the real interest rate returns back to baseline.

---

[114]The literature provides a range of estimates. Summers (1981) estimates χ to equal 16.1. Eberly (1997) estimates linear and nonlinear investment equations on firm-level and aggregate data for 11 industrial countries. Based on aggregate measures constructed from the firm-level data in her sample, she finds estimates for χ between 1.4 and 3. Her instrumental variable estimates for firm-level equations are between 1.75 for Belgium and 9 for the Netherlands. Cummins, Hassett, and Oliner (1997) provide estimates on the order of 5–10 based on firm-level data in the United States.

---

[115]In the first year, the short-term real interest rate falls because the expected increase in the price level more than offsets the increase in the nominal short-term interest rate.

Figure 6. Impulse Responses in Relation to the Investment Block

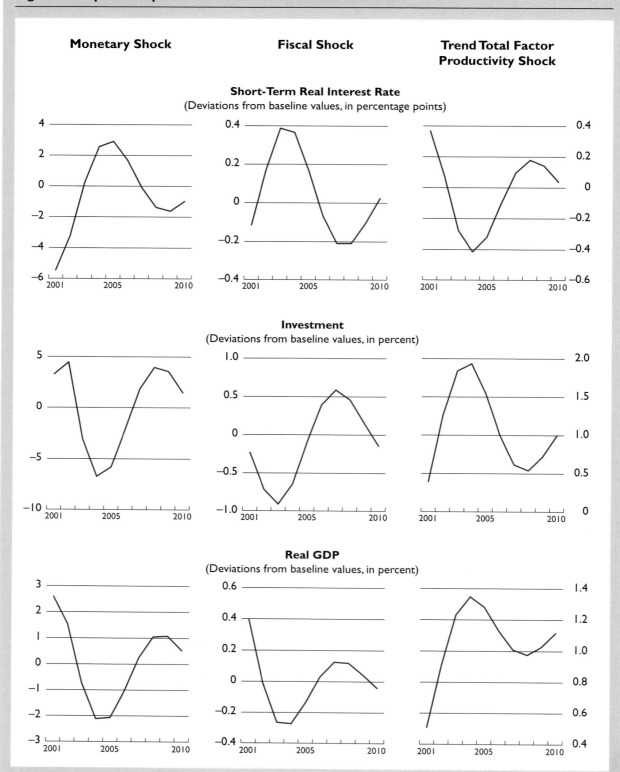

VII International Trade

This section describes the equations that MULTI-MOD uses to explain international trade in countries' main composite goods.[116] The disaggregation of trade flows in the Mark III model remains essentially the same as in Mark II. Imports and exports of goods and nonfactor services are measured according to the national income accounts definition. Imports of oil and non-oil primary commodities, and exports of oil, are then excluded to obtain measures of imports and exports of the main composite goods. A novel feature of Mark III is the use of information from input-output tables (compiled by the OECD) to calculate separate import propensities for consumption, investment, government purchases, and exports. For most countries, the different components of domestic absorption have substantially different import contents. Allowing for these differences enhances MULTIMOD's analysis of the macroeconomic effects, especially on external sector variables, of changes in government expenditure and a variety of other shocks.

Imports

To allow for differences in import propensities for different components of domestic absorption, separate import propensities for each category of absorption (private consumption, private fixed investment, and government purchases) and for exports were calculated using data from the most recent input-output matrices for each country.[117] These import propensities were then used to create weighted measures of aggregate activity (ACT) for each country as follows:

$$ACT_t = \gamma_c C_t + \gamma_G G_t + \gamma_I I_t + \gamma_x X_t. \qquad (59)$$

Figure 7 plots, for each of the major industrial countries and for the block of small industrial countries, the volume of imports as a share of these activity variables, as well as the inverse of the relative price of imports. This figure suggests that, over the last three decades, the trend increase in imports relative to the weighted activity variable has been associated with declines in the price of imports (relative to the price deflator for non-oil GNP). This pattern appears to hold in all cases except for the United States, where import prices rose relatively sharply in the early 1970s.

Table 11 presents estimates of a parsimonious error-correction specification for the import volume equations. This specification reflects the view (supported by Figure 7) that the activity variable and the relative price of imports are likely to be the main determinants of the trend in imports. The parameter γ_{m2} captures the speed of adjustment to the long-run equilibrium relationship. The long-run elasticity of import volumes with respect to the relative price of imports is denoted by the parameter γ_{m3}. The specification also includes changes in the relative price of imports. The parameter γ_{m1} represents the short-run price elasticity of imports. In addition, for countries other than the United States, the regression includes a term specified as the difference between domestic potential output growth and U.S. potential output growth.[118] This term, $F(x)$, allows for the possibility that, in the process of convergence of productivity levels across countries, countries with relatively low productivity levels may have required a transfer of technology in the form of imported investment goods. This term could also reflect the expansion (by foreign producers) of distribution networks for imports, spurred by the expansion of productive capacity abroad.[119]

---

[116]We do not elaborate here on international trade in oil and non-oil primary commodities, which was discussed in Section II.

[117]The OECD has compiled input-output tables for the seven major industrial countries and also for Australia, Denmark, and the Netherlands. The latest versions of these tables (1990 for most countries) were used to compute import propensities for the components of domestic absorption as well as for exports. The last set of numbers reflects exports of goods and services that have a significant content of imported inputs.

[118]Potential output growth rates were computed using smoothed levels of potential output obtained from the World Economic Outlook database.

[119]In the core version of Mark III, this term is turned off in simulation mode. Future extensions of the model will incorporate endogenous total factor productivity growth, along the lines of the analysis in Bayoumi, Coe, and Helpman (1996).

Figure 7. Import-Activity Ratios and Relative Import Prices

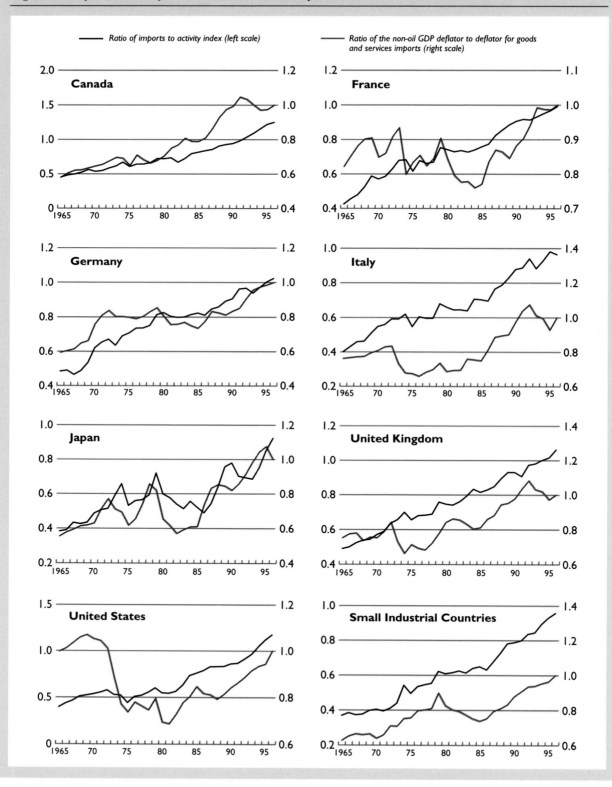

—— Ratio of imports to activity index (left scale)

—— Ratio of the non-oil GDP deflator to deflator for goods and services imports (right scale)

Canada

France

Germany

Italy

Japan

United Kingdom

United States

Small Industrial Countries

Table 11. Volume Equations for Imports

$$\Delta\log(MGSLOC_t) - \Delta\log(ACT_t) = \gamma_{m0} + \gamma_{m1}\,\Delta PMREL_t + \gamma_{m2}\,[\log(MGSLOC_{t-1})$$
$$- \gamma_{m3}\,PMREL_{t-1} - \log ACT_{t-1}] + F(x)$$

MGSLOC: imports of goods and nonfactor services, excluding oil and non-oil commodities.
ACT: weighted activity variable based on import propensities from input-output tables.
F(x): contribution of variables included to control for variation in imports not accounted for by
　　weighted domestic activity and relative prices.[1]
PMREL: relative price of imports in logs.

Estimation period: 1972–96

	γ_{m0}	γ_{m1}	γ_{m2}	γ_{m3}	R^2	SE
Canada	0.01 (0.01)	−0.33** (0.04)	0.06 (0.07)	−0.99** (0.12)	0.56	0.045
France	0.00 (0.01)	−0.33** (0.04)	0.14** (0.05)	−0.99** (0.12)	0.69	0.037
Germany	0.01* (0.01)	−0.33** (0.04)	0.13** (0.05)	−0.99** (0.12)	0.60	0.028
Italy	−0.02 (0.02)	−0.33** (0.04)	0.34** (0.07)	−0.99** (0.12)	0.66	0.048
Japan	−0.07** (0.03)	−0.33** (0.04)	0.35** (0.07)	−0.99** (0.12)	0.56	0.077
United Kingdom	−0.00 (0.01)	−0.33** (0.04)	0.25** (0.05)	−0.99** (0.12)	0.64	0.034
United States	0.03** (0.01)	−0.33** (0.04)	0.06** (0.03)	−0.99** (0.12)	0.73	0.046

Note: Standard errors reported in parentheses. ** (*) indicates statistical significance at the 5 percent (10 percent) level.

[1]For all countries other than the United States, the specification includes the term *F(x)*, defined as domestic potential output growth minus U.S. potential output growth.

Note that the short-run elasticity of imports with respect to activity is constrained to be unity. This restriction, although not supported by the data, is necessary in order to obtain reasonable price elasticities. In the absence of this restriction, the trend in the level of imports would result in estimates of a large elasticity with respect to activity (which also has a trend) and, consequently, a small and often imprecise estimate of the price elasticity.

To minimize the global trade discrepancy (see discussion below), it is assumed that all countries have identical long-run price elasticities. The pooled estimate of this price elasticity (γ_{m3}) is −0.99. The estimated parameters on the error-correction terms (γ_{m2}) vary from a low of 0.06 for Canada and the United States to a high of about 0.35 for Italy and Japan. These parameter estimates are statistically significant for all countries, corroborating the evidence presented in Figure 7 that the upward trend in the volume of imports is associated with the decline in the relative price of imports. The coefficient on the contemporaneous change in relative import prices (γ_{m1}) is also restricted to be the same for all countries. The estimated coefficient is negative and statistically significant.

Import prices are determined in the model as weighted averages of other countries' export prices. The average price of imports of country i, denoted PIM_i, is given by

$$PIM_i = \sum_{j \neq i} s_{ji}(PXM_j E_{ij}), \qquad (60)$$

where s_{ji} denotes the share of exports from country j to country i in the total exports to country i, PXM_j is the price of exports of country j, and E_{ij} is an index of the value of currency j in terms of currency i.

Exports

The econometric specification for the export equation is similar to that of the import equation.

Table 12. Bilateral Total Exports, 1996
(In billions of U.S. dollars)

Exporter	Importer								
	United States	Japan	Germany	Canada	France	Italy	United Kingdom	Smaller industrial countries	Developing countries
United States	—	67.5	23.5	132.6	14.4	8.8	30.9	73.6	271.6
Japan	113.1	—	18.2	5.1	5.4	3.4	12.5	35.9	217.6
Germany	39.9	14.1	—	2.8	55.9	38.1	41.0	188.5	132.6
Canada	164.8	7.5	2.3	—	1.2	1.0	2.8	5.6	15.0
France	17.3	5.4	49.1	1.9	—	26.4	26.9	92.6	68.3
Italy	18.4	5.6	43.7	1.8	31.4	—	16.2	60.1	73.6
United Kingdom	31.4	6.7	29.5	3.1	24.2	11.5	—	84.0	68.0
Smaller industrial countries	53.9	31.8	183.5	7.6	100.6	51.1	91.1	240.9	205.2
Developing countries	365.2	180.9	103.1	20.6	56.1	50.1	65.7	178.4	716.7

The scale variable used in this equation is foreign activity, and the relative price variable is the real competitiveness index (*RCI*).

The foreign activity variable is constructed as a weighted sum of the import volumes of other countries. The weights are equal to the base period shares of the home country's exports accounted for by the foreign countries and are based on the pattern of trade flows in 1996; see Table 12.

The real competitiveness index (*RCI*) is defined as a weighted sum of the logarithms of export prices of a country's trading partners relative to home-country export prices. This competitiveness index is constructed in a manner consistent with the use of partner countries' imports as the foreign activity variable that enters into the export equations.[120]

Consider the following identity that relates the exports of a given country (X_i) to the imports of each of its trading partners (M_j), weighted by its share in each of their markets (s_{ij}):

$$X_i \equiv \sum_{j \neq i} s_{ij} M_j. \qquad (61)$$

The base-period export share of country i to country j is denoted by

$$\bar{x}_{ij} = \left(\frac{\bar{M}_j}{\bar{X}_i} \right) \bar{s}_{ij}, \qquad (62)$$

where the bar above a variable indicates the base-period value of that variable. It can then be shown that an appropriate set of weights for constructing country i's competitiveness index is as follows:[121]

$$w_{ik} = \sum_{j \neq i, k} \bar{x}_{ij} \bar{s}_{kj}, \quad i \neq k$$
$$w_{ii} = -\sum_{k \neq i} w_{ik}. \qquad (63)$$

The weights w_{ik} indicate the sensitivity of the exports of country i to competition in third markets from country k. The weights are normalized to sum to one for each country. The foreign activity variable for country i is defined as follows:

$$FACT_i = \sum_{j \neq i} \bar{s}_{ij} \bar{M}_j \bar{E}_{ij}, \qquad (64)$$

where $\bar{E}_{ij}$ denotes the base-period price of currency j in terms of currency i.

The export volume equation is specified in first differences but includes an error-correction term. The estimated export equations constrain the coefficients on the lagged level of the real exchange rate to be the same for all countries. Also, the short-run elasticity of exports with respect to foreign activity is constrained to be unity. This restriction is imposed since, as in the import equation, the elasticity of ex-

---

[120]Measures of nominal and real effective exchange rates based on direct trade shares are also computed in the model. These weights take into account competition in third markets and also the differences among countries in the relative importance of international trade. The methodology for computing the weights is similar to that of the IMF's Information Notice System described in McGuirk (1987) and Zanello and Desruelle (1997).

---

[121]See Meredith (1997) for details on the derivation of these weights.

Table 13. Volume Equations for Exports

$$\Delta \log (XGSLO_t) - \Delta \log (FACT_t) = \gamma_{X0} + \gamma_{X1} \Delta \log (RCI_t) + \gamma_{X2}[\log (XGSLO_{t-1}) - \gamma_{X3} \log (RCI_{t-1}) - \log (FACT_{t-1})]$$

XGSLO: exports of goods and nonfactor services, excluding oil.
FACT: weighted sum of import volumes in other countries/regions.
RCI: real competitiveness index.

Estimation period: 1972–96

	γ_{x0}	γ_{x1}	γ_{x2}	γ_{x3}	R^2	SE
Canada	−0.00 (0.01)	−0.41** (0.10)	0.01 (0.01)	−1.74** (0.29)	0.76	0.032
France	0.00 (0.01)	−0.48** (0.08)	0.01 (0.03)	−1.74** (0.29)	0.64	0.028
Germany	−0.00 (0.01)	−0.40** (0.07)	0.06* (0.03)	−1.74** (0.29)	0.57	0.033
Italy	−0.02** (0.01)	−0.38** (0.10)	0.17** (0.06)	−1.74** (0.29)	0.50	0.035
Japan	−0.02** (0.01)	−0.45** (0.11)	0.36** (0.09)	−1.74** (0.29)	0.46	0.044
United Kingdom	0.00 (0.01)	−0.45** (0.08)	0.13** (0.03)	−1.74** (0.29)	0.72	0.025
United States	0.03** (0.01)	−0.42** (0.06)	0.08** (0.02)	−1.74** (0.29)	0.77	0.026

Note: Standard errors reported in parentheses. ** (*) indicates statistical significance at the 5 percent (10 percent) level.

ports with respect to foreign activity would otherwise be dominated by the trends in these two variables and result in very low estimates of the price elasticity.

Estimates of the export volume equations are presented in Table 13. The long-run price elasticity of exports (γ_{x3}) is estimated to be −1.74. Short-run price elasticities (γ_{x1}) differ across countries and are lower than the long-run price elasticity, but are still quite large and statistically significant for all countries. The estimated parameters on the error-correction terms (γ_{x2}) are positive in all cases and statistically significant for all countries except Canada and France. This suggests that, in the long run, exports are generally closely tied to the foreign activity and real exchange rate variables. This is confirmed by Figure 8, which plots, for each country, the ratio of export volume to the foreign activity variable as well as the real competitiveness index.

Export price equations were estimated for the major industrial countries. The rate of change of export prices is assumed to be linearly related to the rates of change of the price of domestic non-oil output and the prices of foreign non-oil exports, where foreign prices use the same weighting scheme as the

real competitiveness index, reflecting competition in all export markets. In addition, the lagged logarithmic difference between domestic prices and home-country export prices is included in the specification, thereby forcing export prices to change in proportion to the change in domestic output prices over the long run. The coefficient on this term was restricted to be the same for all countries; this restriction was not rejected by the data. The estimates of the export price equations are reported in Table 14. The sensitivity of export prices to the rate of change of foreign prices is quite similar across the major industrial countries.

Adding Up of World Trade and Current Account Balances

The existence of a global trade discrepancy, which implies that exports and imports summed across all countries are not equal, is a well-known problem. The discrepancy is even larger when the current account, which includes factor incomes, is aggregated across all countries. Although such a discrepancy might exist in the baseline, it is desirable for the

Figure 8. Export-Activity Ratios and Real Competitiveness Indices

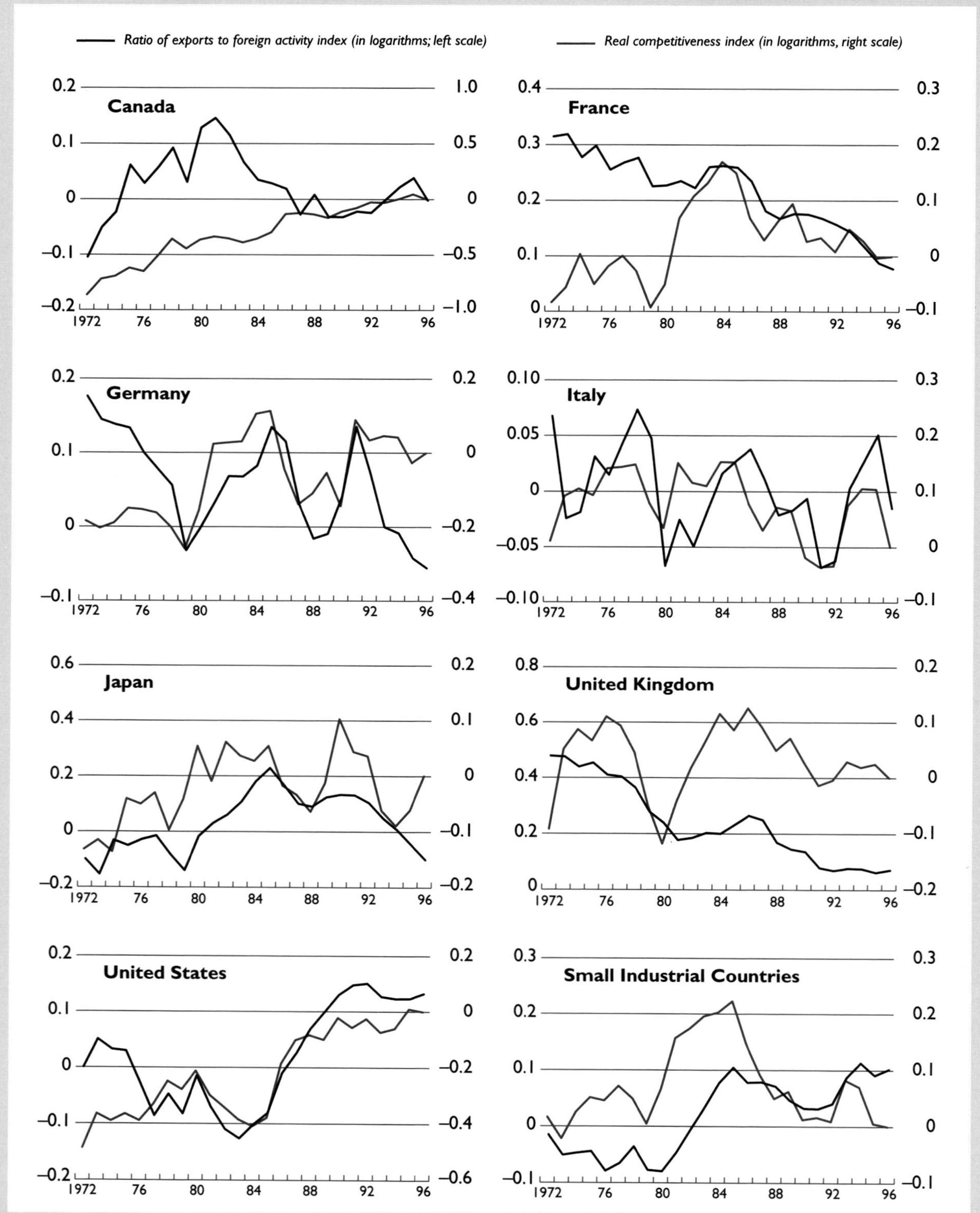

——— Ratio of exports to foreign activity index (in logarithms; left scale)   ——— Real competitiveness index (in logarithms, right scale)

Table 14. Export Price Equations

$$\Delta \log(PXM_t) = \gamma_{px0} + \gamma_{px1}\, \Delta \log(PGNPNO_t)$$
$$+ (1 - \gamma_{px1})\, \Delta \log(PFM_t)$$
$$+ \gamma_{px2} \log(PGNPNO_{t-1}/PXM_{t-1})$$

PXM: export price of the composite good that excludes oil and primary commodities.

PGNPNO: non-oil GDP deflator.

PFM: a weighted average of competitors' prices in foreign markets.

	γ_{px0}	γ_{px1}	γ_{px2}	R^2	SE
Canada	−0.01*	0.64**	0.03**	0.59	0.032
	(0.01)	(0.05)	(0.01)		
France	−0.00	0.71**	0.03**	0.92	0.016
	(0.00)	(0.03)	(0.01)		
Germany	−0.00	0.81**	0.03**	0.17	0.047
	(0.01)	(0.10)	(0.01)		
Italy	0.00	0.66**	0.03**	0.90	0.024
	(0.00)	(0.05)	(0.01)		
Japan	−0.00	0.65**	0.03**	0.92	0.028
	(0.01)	(0.02)	(0.01)		
United Kingdom	−0.00	0.63**	0.03**	0.87	0.019
	(0.00)	(0.04)	(0.01)		
United States	−0.00	0.64**	0.03**	0.54	0.034
	(0.01)	(0.04)	(0.01)		

Note: Standard errors reported in parentheses. ** (*) indicates statistical significance at the 5 percent (10 percent) level.

model to have the property that incremental exports and imports be equal.

The new weighting scheme used to construct the price and activity variables for the trade equations ensures that this discrepancy is very small, although not exactly zero. Adding up of world trade is, therefore, imposed by allocating real and nominal trade discrepancies to export volumes and import prices, respectively.[122] Given the adding up of world trade, the adding up of current account balances across all countries is then imposed on the simulations by constructing estimates of net foreign asset positions that sum to zero globally and by assuming that all claims pay the same U.S. dollar interest rate.[123]

---

[122]The model contains equations for adjusted exports that are equal to unadjusted exports, determined using the export equations described above, plus, for each country, a coefficient times the excess relative to baseline of world import volumes over export volumes. This coefficient reflects the share of the country in total world trade in goods and nonfactor services excluding oil. The remaining discrepancy in nominal trade flows is allocated across countries in a similar fashion by adjusting import prices.

[123]As described in Masson, Symansky, and Meredith (1990), for all countries and country groups except the main developing country bloc, estimates of net foreign asset positions are constructed by cumulating measured current account balances. The net foreign asset position of the main developing country bloc is then constructed as a residual.

VIII   Extensions of the Core Model

This section describes a number of extensions of the standard version of MULTIMOD Mark III and discusses their applications. The objective is to provide a flavor of the ease with which the model can be modified to analyze specific issues of topical interest. The virtue of keeping the core model simple and transparent in order to facilitate various modifications becomes apparent.

The extensions of the model can be divided into two broad and interrelated categories. The first category relates to the construction of specific models for individual countries or country groups that, in the core version of MULTIMOD, are aggregated with other countries or country groups. These models can be used to analyze the effects of employing parameters or incorporating macroeconomic features that are specific to a particular country (or group of countries), or to analyze the effects of shocks that impinge on a particular country. The second category involves modifications of the structure of the model in order to analyze broader macroeconomic policy issues.

Extensions of Country Coverage

As noted in earlier sections, small industrial countries are aggregated into a single block in the core version of MULTIMOD. It is, however, quite straightforward to construct a model for a specific small industrial economy under the maintained assumption that the macroeconomic structure of these economies is similar to that of larger industrial economies. Certain aspects do, however, need to be considered carefully for each country. The degree of openness to international trade needs to be accounted for properly in order to capture the dynamics of foreign trade and external debt variables, both of which are typically crucial for economic activity in these countries. Since the effects of domestic policy actions on external sector variables could have important implications for domestic price and activity variables, these relationships should ideally be estimated individually for the country under consideration. Other variables, such as the capital-output

---

> **Box 10. Steps Necessary to Integrate Additional Industrial Countries**
>
> - Develop a database from various sources, including the *World Economic Outlook* and OECD analytical databases, and develop a new trade matrix for the country disaggregation that is being chosen.
> - Modify the program that creates the equations for the dynamic and steady-state models.
> - Update the estimation programs and include the additional country codes to obtain estimates of the behavioral parameters for the added countries. If the parameter estimates are judged to be nonsensical—which is sometimes the case with small data samples, regime changes, and so on—impose pooled estimates or values obtained from other countries that have similar structures.
> - Develop a baseline that includes history, the *World Economic Outlook* projection, and convergence to a steady-state balanced growth path.
> - Modify the reporting system that generates standard MULTIMOD graphs and tables.
> - Run standard tests to check the consistency of the dynamic and steady-state models.
> - Run standard shocks on the individual country models as well as the full model.

---

ratio, should also be calibrated based on country-specific estimates.

The parameterization of a model of a small country can easily accommodate country-specific estimates of the main model parameters. For certain parameters, however, country-specific estimates may be imprecise, and pooled estimates from multicountry estimation might be preferred. This decision is left to the judgment of the modeler. Alternative specifications of certain equations can also be accommodated, although care should be taken to ensure that the accounting identities in the model are respected.

The operational procedure for building a small industrial country model is very straightforward—Box 10 provides a summary of the steps that are necessary to add an individual country model. To extract a country from the bloc of small industrial countries and create a separate model for it, the first step would be to subtract from the bloc the macroeconomic aggregates related to this country. For instance, real GDP in the bloc of small industrial countries would be redefined by subtracting out the real GDP of this country. Next, the trade variables would have to be redefined in a manner that ensured consistency in the world trade matrix, and the appropriate weights for constructing the country's real competitiveness index and real effective exchange rate would have to be computed. Finally, the model code for the large industrial economies would then be replicated for the small industrial country, employing country-specific or average parameters for the small industrial countries as appropriate. Thus, at the end of this process, the enhanced version of MULTIMOD would have a similar structure as the original model, but with one additional country.

In most contexts, it is relatively easy to justify the assumption that small countries have negligible effects on other economies or, more generally, on the rest of the world. The computational complexities of the model are reduced substantially in this case because the model of the small country can then be simulated in isolation without allowing for feedback effects on the rest of the world, that is, by keeping conditions in the other country blocs constant.

An interesting example of recent work in this direction is that of Laxton and Prasad (1997), who construct a model of the Swiss economy in order to examine the possible short-term consequences of European Economic and Monetary Union for Switzerland. A number of enhancements to the core model were required for this analysis. For instance, with official short-term nominal interest rates in 1997 at less than 100 basis points, the potency of monetary policy was severely constrained. To capture the effects of the nominal interest floor at zero percent, a nonlinear money demand specification for Switzerland was estimated and adopted in this analysis. The interactions between this nonlinearity and the convexity of the Phillips curve turn out to have interesting policy implications.

There is, of course, no technical limitation on the number of small country models that can be inserted into the core model, although care needs to be exercised about modeling the interactions among these economies. One example of such an exercise is provided by Masson and Turtelboom (1997). These authors create country-specific models for each of the 15 countries of the European Union (except for Luxembourg, which is modeled jointly with Belgium) and then perform stochastic simulations of the model in order to examine the relative variability of macroeconomic variables under different assumptions about monetary arrangements within this group of countries.

Work has also commenced on separating a group of emerging market economies from the main developing country model. In the analysis for the December 1997 *World Economic Outlook,* an emerging market bloc was created, with a model structure analogous to that for industrial countries, in order to examine the global effects of a cutback in net capital flows to the emerging markets.

Other Modifications

The extensions discussed above have focused on modifying MULTIMOD to tackle issues that are best addressed with a different set of country groups than those contained in the core Mark III version. In other applications, the basic structure of MULTIMOD has been modified, without extending the country coverage, to enhance the analysis of various policy issues. The examples discussed below illustrate that the model is flexible enough to incorporate advances in economic theory that relate to key elements of the model's structure. Analyzing the implications of different policy scenarios when such features are included in the model can often be quite revealing.

Fiscal Consolidation

The core version of MULTIMOD can be used to examine the effects of fiscal restructuring and to compare the macroeconomic effects of changes in alternative fiscal instruments. Revenue and expenditure measures that have similar effects on the fiscal balance could have markedly different macroeconomic effects, both in the short run and in the long run. Further, the potentially larger distortionary effects of direct taxes compared with indirect taxes suggest that the composition of revenue measures could also be important. Similarly, reductions in government investment could have very different effects on long-term growth than reductions in current government expenditures.

MULTIMOD can be modified quite easily to focus on these issues. For instance, Bartolini, Razin, and Symansky (1995) incorporate an extended set of fiscal instruments in MULTIMOD to examine differences in the effects of the composition of fiscal consolidation measures in the seven major industrial countries. By introducing distortionary effects of taxation, they are able to demonstrate clear differences in the short-run and long-run output and welfare effects of expenditure reductions, increases in indirect taxes, and increases in taxes on factor income.

Another important consideration when examining the effects of fiscal consolidation is the degree of credibility associated with such a consolidation effort. The forward-looking behavior of economic agents that is captured in MULTIMOD is clearly crucial for such an exercise. Bayoumi and Laxton (1994) use MULTIMOD to analyze the effects of debt reduction in Canada under different credibility scenarios. Their simulations underscore the importance of credibility as well as coordination between the fiscal and monetary authorities. This points to another strength of MULTIMOD—the ability to analyze the joint effects of different policy instruments on macroeconomic variables.

Endogenous Productivity Growth

One of the main developments in the economic growth literature in recent years has been the theory of endogenous growth (see, for example, Lucas, 1988 and Romer, 1990). Bayoumi, Coe, and Helpman (1996) extend MULTIMOD in this direction by allowing for externalities in the form of international spillovers of research and development (R&D) expenditures on total factor productivity growth. The role of international trade in facilitating these spillover effects and the interplay between R&D spending and capital investment are highlighted in their simulations, which also provide quantitative estimates of the effects of country-specific R&D spending on output growth in the global economy.[124]

---

[124]The Mark III version of MULTIMOD has also been extended to allow for endogenous total factor productivity—see Bayoumi, Coe, and Laxton (1998).

This example illustrates how recent developments in economic theory can be embedded in MULTIMOD. The model enables researchers to carefully analyze the quantitative importance of the overall effects of factors such as R&D spillovers, as well as the channels through which these effects permeate.

Military Expenditures

Another extension that highlights the usefulness of MULTIMOD in providing quantitative answers to interesting policy questions is provided by Bayoumi, Hewitt, and Schiff (1993). These authors explore the macroeconomic effects of a reduction in world military expenditures and show that, in the long run, the welfare effects of reductions in military spending can be quite large. In a related paper, Bayoumi, Hewitt, and Symansky (1995) show that these welfare gains can be even larger for developing countries and, by disaggregating these countries into four geographic groups, provide estimates of how much each of these groups of countries stands to gain from reductions in military expenditures.

In addition to the examples discussed above, numerous other extensions of MULTIMOD have been used in recent years to address a broad class of policy-related issues. Notwithstanding the substantial recent improvements incorporated into the core Mark III model, the sophisticated yet transparent and versatile structure of MULTIMOD remains one of its main virtues.

References

Adams, Charles, and David T. Coe, 1990, "A Systems Approach to Estimating the Natural Rate of Unemployment and Potential Output for the United States," *Staff Papers,* International Monetary Fund, Vol. 37 (June), pp. 232–93.

Akerlof, George, William Dickens, and George Perry, 1996, "The Macroeconomics of Low Inflation," *Brookings Papers on Economic Activity: 1,* Brookings Institution, pp. 1–76.

Armstrong, J., R. Black, D. Laxton, and D. Rose, "A Robust Method for Simulating Forward-Looking Models," *Journal of Economic Dynamics and Control,* forthcoming.

Attanasio, O.P., and G. Weber, 1993, "Consumption Growth, the Interest Rate, and Aggregation," *Review of Economic Studies,* Vol. 60 (July), pp. 631–99.

Australia, Commonwealth Treasury, 1996, Documentation of the Treasury Macroeconomic (TRYM) Model of the Australian Economy (Canberra, Australia: Commonwealth Treasury).

Ball, Laurence M., and Gregory Mankiw, 1994, "A Sticky-Price Manifesto," NBER Working Paper No. 4677 (Cambridge, Massachusetts: National Bureau of Economic Research).

Barr, David G., and John Y. Campbell, 1996, "Inflation, Real Interest Rates, and the Bond Market: A Study of UK Nominal and Index-Linked Government Bond Prices," NBER Working Paper No. 5821 (Cambridge, Massachusetts: National Bureau of Economic Research).

Barro, R.J., 1974, "Are Government Bonds Net Wealth?" *Journal of Political Economy,* Vol. 82 (November/December), pp. 1095–117.

———, 1989, "The Ricardian Approach to Budget Deficits," *Journal of Economic Perspectives,* Vol. 3 (Spring), pp. 37–54.

Bartolini, Leonardo, Asaf Razin, and Steven Symansky, 1995, "G-7 Fiscal Restructuring in the 1990s: Macroeconomic Effects," *Economic Policy,* Vol. 20 (April), pp. 111–46.

Bayoumi, Tamim, David T. Coe, and Douglas Laxton, 1998, "Liberating Supply: Technological Innovation in a Multicountry Econometric Model" (unpublished; Washington: International Monetary Fund).

Bayoumi, Tamim, David T. Coe, and Elhanan Helpman, 1996, "R&D Spillovers and Global Growth," IMF Working Paper 96/47 (Washington: International Monetary Fund).

Bayoumi, Tamim, Daniel Hewitt, and Steven Symansky, 1995, "MULTIMOD Simulations of the Effects on Developing Countries of Decreasing Military Spending," in *North-South Linkages and International Macroeconomic Policy,* ed. by David Vines and David Currie (Cambridge; New York: Cambridge University Press).

Bayoumi, Tamim, and Douglas Laxton, 1994, "Government Deficits, Debt, and the Business Cycle," in *Deficit Reduction—What Pain, What Gain?* ed. by William B.P. Robson and William M. Scarth (Toronto: C.D. Howe Institute).

Bayoumi, Tamim, Daniel Hewitt, and Jerald Schiff, 1993, "Economic Consequences of Lower Military Spending: Some Simulation Results," IMF Working Paper 93/17 (Washington: International Monetary Fund, March).

Bean, Charles, 1996, "The Convex Phillips Curve and Macroeconomic Policymaking Under Uncertainty" (unpublished; London: HM Treasury).

Bernheim, B.D., 1989, "A Neoclassical Perspective on Budget Deficits," *Journal of Economic Perspectives,* Vol. 3 (Spring), pp. 55–72.

———, and K. Bagwell, 1988, "Is Everything Neutral?" *Journal of Political Economy,* Vol. 96 (April), pp. 308–38.

Bertola, Giuseppe, 1988, "Adjustment Costs and Dynamic Factor Demands: Investment and Employment Under Uncertainty" (Ph.D. dissertation; Cambridge, Massachusetts: Massachusetts Institute of Technology).

———, and Ricardo J. Caballero, 1990, "Kinked Adjustment Costs and Aggregate Dynamics," in *NBER Macroeconomics Annual,* ed. by Olivier Blanchard and Stanley Fischer (Cambridge, Massachusetts: MIT Press).

Black, Richard, V. Cassino, A. Drew, E. Hansen, B. Hunt, D. Rose, and A. Scott, 1997, "The Forecasting and Policy System: The Core Model," Research Paper No. 43 (Wellington, New Zealand: Reserve Bank of New Zealand).

Black, Richard, D. Laxton, D. Rose, and R. Tetlow, 1994, "The Steady-State Model: SSQPM," *The Bank of Canada's New Quarterly Projection Model,* Bank of Canada Technical Report No. 72, Part 1.

Blanchard, Olivier J., 1985, "Debt, Deficits and Finite Horizons," *Journal of Political Economy,* Vol. 93 (April), pp. 223–47.

———, and Stanley Fischer, 1989, *Lectures on Macroeconomics* (Cambridge, Massachusetts: MIT Press).

Blanchard, Olivier J., and D. Quah, 1989, "The Dynamic Effects of Aggregate Supply and Demand Disturbances," *American Economic Review,* Vol. 79 (September), pp. 655–73.

Blanchard, Olivier J., and Lawrence F. Katz, 1997, "What We Know and Do Not Know About the Natural Rate of Unemployment," in *Journal of Economic Perspectives,* Vol. 11 (Winter), pp. 51–72.

Blanchard, Olivier J., and Lawrence Summers, 1986, "Hysteresis and the European Unemployment Problem," in *NBER Macroeconomics Annual,* ed. by S. Fischer (Cambridge, Massachusetts; London, United Kingdom: MIT Press).

Bond, Stephen, and Costas Meghir, 1994, "Dynamic Investment Models and the Firm's Financial Policy," *Review of Economic Studies,* Vol. 61 (April), pp. 197–222.

Bos, Eduard, My T. Vu, Earnest Massiah, and Rudolfo A. Bulatao, 1994, *World Population Projections, 1994–95 Edition* (Baltimore, Maryland: Published for the World Bank by the Johns Hopkins University Press).

Boucekkine, R., 1995, "An Alternative Methodology for Solving Nonlinear Forward-Looking Models," in *Journal of Economic Dynamics and Control,* Vol. 19, No. 4, pp. 711–34.

Bryant, Ralph, 1996, "Alternative Rules for Monetary Policy and Fiscal Policy in New Zealand: A Preliminary Assessment of Stabilization Properties," Brookings Discussion Papers in International Economics, No. 127 (July).

———, and Long Zhang, 1996a, "Intertemporal Fiscal Policy in Macroeconomic Models: Introduction and Major Alternatives," Brookings Discussion Papers in International Economics, No. 123 (June).

———, 1996b, "Alternative Specifications of Intertemporal Fiscal Policy in a Small Theoretical Model," Brookings Discussion Papers in International Economics, No. 124 (June).

Bryant, R., P. Hooper, and C. Mann, eds., 1993, *Evaluating Policy Regimes: New Research in Empirical Macroeconomics* (Washington: Brookings Institution).

Buiter, Willem H., 1988, "Death, Birth, Productivity Growth and Debt Neutrality," *Economic Journal,* Vol. 98 (June), pp. 279–93.

———, and Marcus Miller, 1985, "Costs and Benefits of an Anti-Inflationary Policy: Questions and Issues," in *Inflation and Unemployment: Theory, Experience and Policy-Making,* ed. by V. Argy and J. Nevile (London: George Allen & Unwin).

Callen, Tim, and Doug Laxton, 1998, "A Small Macro Model of the Australian Inflation Process with Endogenous Policy Credibility" (unpublished; Washington: International Monetary Fund).

Calvo, Guillermo A., 1983, "Staggered Prices in a Utility-Maximizing Framework," *Journal of Monetary Economics,* Vol. 12 (September), pp. 383–98.

Chadha, Bankim, Paul Masson, and Guy Meredith, 1992, "Models of Inflation and the Costs of Disinflation," *Staff Papers,* International Monetary Fund, Vol. 39 (June), pp. 395–431.

Clark, Peter B., and Douglas Laxton, 1997, "Phillips Curves, Phillips Lines and the Unemployment Costs of Overheating," IMF Working Paper 97/17 (Washington: International Monetary Fund).

———, and Rose, 1996, "Asymmetry in the U.S. Output-Inflation Nexus," *Staff Papers,* International Monetary Fund, Vol. 43 (March), pp. 216–51.

———, 1995, "Capacity Constraints, Inflation, and the Transmission Mechanism: Forward-Looking Versus Myopic Policy Rules," IMF Working Paper 95/75 (Washington: International Monetary Fund).

Coletti, D., B. Hunt, David Rose, and Robert Tetlow, 1996, "The Dynamic Model: QPM," in *The Bank of Canada's New Quarterly Projection Model,* Part 3, Technical Report No. 75 (Ottawa: Bank of Canada).

Cummins, Jason, Kevin Hassett, and Stephen Oliner, 1997, "Investment Behavior, Observable Expectations, and Internal Funds" (unpublished; New York: New York University).

Debelle, Guy, and Douglas Laxton, 1997, "Is the Phillips Curve Really a Curve? Some Evidence for Canada, the United Kingdom, and the United States," *Staff Papers,* International Monetary Fund, Vol. 44 (June), pp. 249–82.

Debelle, Guy, and James Vickery, 1997, "Is the Phillips Curve a Curve? Some Evidence and Implications for Australia" (unpublished; Sydney, Australia: Reserve Bank of Australia, Economic Research Department).

De Long, J.B., 1996, "America's Only Peacetime Inflation: The 1970s," NBER Historical Working Paper No. 084 (Cambridge, Massachusetts: National Bureau of Economic Research).

———, and L.H. Summers, 1988, "How Does Macroeconomic Policy Affect Output?" *Brookings Papers on Economic Activity*: 2, Brookings Institution, pp. 433–80.

Diamond, Peter A., 1965, "National Debt in a Neoclassical Growth Model," *American Economic Review,* Vol. 55 (December), pp. 1126–50.

Dixit, A., and R.S. Pindyck, 1994, *Investment Under Uncertainty* (Princeton, N.J.: Princeton University Press).

Duesenberry, James, and others, eds., 1965, *The Brookings Quarterly Econometric Model of the United States* (Chicago: Rand McNally).

Dupasquier, C., and N. Ricketts, 1997, "Non-linearities in the Output-Inflation Relationship," paper presented at the Bank of Canada Conference on Price Stability, Inflation Targets and Monetary Policy.

Eberly, Janice, 1997, "International Evidence on Investment and Fundamentals," *European Economic Review,* Vol. 41 (June), pp. 1055–78.

Edison, H.J., J.R. Marquez, and R.W. Tryon, 1987, "The Structure and Properties of the Federal Reserve Board Multicountry Model," *Economic Modelling,* Vol. 4 (April), pp. 115–315.

Epstein, Larry G., and Michael G. Denny, 1983, "The Multivariate Flexible Accelerator Model: Its Empirical Restrictions and an Application to U.S. Manufacturing," *Econometrica,* Vol. 51 (May), pp. 647–74.

Ericsson, Neil, and John Irons, 1995, "The Lucas Critique in Practice: Theory Without Evidence," in *Macroeco-*

nomics: Developments, Tensions, and Prospects, ed. by K. Hoover (Boston: Kluwer Academic).

Evans, Martin, and Paul Wachtel, 1993, "Inflation Regimes and the Sources of Inflation Uncertainty," *Journal of Money, Credit and Banking,* Vol. 25 (August), pp. 475–511.

Evans, Paul, 1991, "Is Ricardian Equivalence a Good Approximation?" *Economic Inquiry,* Vol. 29 (October), pp. 624–44.

Fair, Ray, and John Taylor, 1983, "Solution and Maximum Likelihood Estimation of Dynamic Nonlinear Rational Expectations Models," *Econometrica,* Vol. 51 (July), pp. 1169–85.

Faruqee, Hamid, Douglas Laxton, and David Rose, 1998, "Inflation and Unemployment in Europe and North America: Asymmetry Versus Hysteresis" (unpublished; Washington: International Monetary Fund).

Faruqee, Hamid, Douglas Laxton, and Steve Symansky, 1997, "Government Debt, Life-Cycle Income and Liquidity Constraints: Beyond Approximate Ricardian Equivalence," *Staff Papers,* International Monetary Fund, Vol. 44 (September), pp. 374–82.

Fisher, P.G., L. Mahadeva, and J.D. Whitley, 1996, "The Output Gap and Inflation-Experience at The Bank of England," paper presented at a meeting of BIS Model Builders, November.

Fischer, Stanley, 1977, "Long-term Contracts, Rational Expectations, and the Optimal Money Supply Rule," *Journal of Political Economy,* Vol. 85 (February), pp. 191–205.

———, 1994, "Modern Central Banking," in *The Future of Central Banking,* ed. by F. Capie and others (Cambridge, United Kingdom; New York, N.Y.: Cambridge University Press).

Ford, Robert, and Douglas Laxton, 1995, "World Public Debt and Real Interest Rates," IMF Working Paper 95/30 (Washington: International Monetary Fund).

Ford, Robert, and David Rose, 1989, "Estimates of the NAIRU Using an Extended Okun's Law," Working Paper No. 89–3 (Ottawa: Bank of Canada).

Friedman, Milton, 1968, "The Role of Monetary Policy," *American Economic Review,* Vol. 58 (March), pp. 1–17.

Fuhrer, Jeffrey C., and George R. Moore, 1995, "Monetary Policy Trade-Offs and the Correlation Between Nominal Interest Rates and Real Output," *American Economic Review,* Vol. 85 (March), pp. 219–39.

Gagnon, Joseph E., 1991, "A Forward-Looking Multicountry Model for Policy Analysis: MX3," *Economic and Financial Computing,* Vol. 1 (Winter), pp. 311–61.

———, 1996, "Long Memory in Inflation Expectations: Evidence from International Financial Markets," International Finance Discussion Paper No. 538 (Washington: United States Board of Governors of the Federal Reserve, International Finance Division).

Goodfriend, Marvin, 1993, "Interest Rate Policy and the Inflation Scare Problem: 1979–1992," *Economic Quarterly,* Federal Reserve Bank of Richmond, Vol. 79 (Winter), pp. 1–24.

Haas, Richard, and Paul Masson, 1986, "MINIMOD: Specification and Simulation Results," *Staff Papers,* International Monetary Fund, Vol. 33 (December), pp. 722–67.

Hall, Robert E., 1988, "Intertemporal Substitution in Consumption," *Journal of Political Economy,* Vol. 96 (December), pp. 330–57.

Helliwell, John F., 1993, "Comment," in *Evaluating Policy Regimes: New Research in Empirical Macroeconomics,* ed. by R. Bryant, P. Hooper, and C. Mann (Washington: Brookings Institution), pp. 416–25.

———, Guy Meredith, P. Bagnoli, and Y. Durand, 1990, "INTERMOD 1.1: A G-7 Version of the IMF's Multimod," *Economic Modelling,* Vol. 7 (January), pp. 3–62.

Hodrick, Robert J., and Edward C. Prescott, 1981, "Post-War U.S. Business Cycles: An Empirical Investigation," Carnegie-Mellon Discussion Paper No. 451 (Pittsburgh: Carnegie-Mellon University).

Hollinger, P., 1996, "The Stacked-Time Simulator in TROLL: A Robust Algorithm for Solving Forward-Looking Models," paper presented at the Second International Conference on Computing in Economics and Finance (Geneva, Switzerland).

International Monetary Fund, 1996, *World Economic Outlook, May 1996: A Study by the Staff of the International Monetary Fund* (Washington).

Isard, Peter, and Douglas Laxton, 1996, "Strategic Choice in Phillips Curve Specification: What If Bob Gordon Is Wrong?" (unpublished; Washington: International Monetary Fund).

Jappelli, T., and M. Pagano, 1989, "Consumption and Capital Market Imperfections: An International Comparison," *American Economic Review,* Vol. 79 (December), pp. 1088–105.

Juillard, Michel, 1996, DYNARE: "A Program for the Resolution and Simulation of Dynamic Models with Forward Variables Through the Use of a Relaxation Algorithm," CEPREMAP Working Paper No. 9602 (Paris, France).

———, and Douglas Laxton, 1996, "A Robust and Efficient Method for Solving Nonlinear Rational Expectations Models," IMF Working Paper No. 96/106 (Washington: International Monetary Fund).

———, Peter McAdam, and Hope Pioro, 1998, "An Algorithm Competition: First-Order Iterations Versus Newton-Based Techniques," *Journal of Economic Dynamics and Control.*

Keynes, John M., 1936, *The General Theory of Employment, Interest and Money* (New York: Harcourt, Brace and World).

Klein, Lawrence, and Arthur Goldberger, 1955, *An Econometric Model of the United States, 1929–1952* (Amsterdam: North-Holland).

Klein, Lawrence, R.J. Ball, A. Hazelwood, and P. Vandome, 1961, *An Econometric Model of the United Kingdom* (Oxford: Blackwell).

Kuttner, Kenneth N., 1992, "Monetary Policy with Uncertain Estimates of Potential Output," *Economic Perspectives,* Reserve Bank of Chicago (January–February), pp. 2–15.

———, 1994, "Estimating Potential Output as a Latent Variable," *Journal of Business and Economic Statistics,* Vol. 12 (July), pp. 361–68.

Laffargue, J.P., 1990, "Résolution d'un Modèle Macroéconomique avec Anticipations Rationnelles," *Annales d'Economie et de Statistique,* Institut National de la Statistique et des Etudes, Vol. 17 (January–March), pp. 97–119.

Laxton, Douglas, and Eswar Prasad, 1997, "Possible Effects of European Monetary Union on Switzerland: A Case Study of Policy Dilemmas Caused by Low Inflation and the Nominal Interest Rate Floor," IMF Working Paper 97/23 (Washington: International Monetary Fund).

Laxton, Douglas, Guy Meredith, and David Rose, 1995, "Asymmetric Effects of Economic Activity on Inflation: Evidence and Policy Implications," *Staff Papers,* International Monetary Fund, Vol. 42 (June), pp. 344–74.

Laxton, Douglas, Nicholas Ricketts, and David Rose, 1994, "Uncertainty, Learning and Policy Credibility," in *Economic Behavior and Policy Choice Under Price Stability* (Ottawa: Bank of Canada).

Laxton, Douglas, David Rose, and Demosthenes Tambakis, 1998, "The U.S. Phillips Curve: The Case for Asymmetry," forthcoming, IMF Working Paper (Washington: International Monetary Fund).

Laxton, Douglas, David Rose, and Robert Tetlow, 1993, "Is the Canadian Phillips Curve Nonlinear?" Working Paper 93-7 (Ottawa: Bank of Canada).

Laxton, Douglas, and Robert Tetlow, 1992, "Government Debt in an Open Economy," Technical Report No. 58 (Ottawa: Bank of Canada).

Layard, Richard, Stephen Nickell, and Richard Jackman, 1991, *Unemployment: Macro-economic Performance and the Labour Market* (Oxford; New York: Oxford University Press).

Levin, Andrew, John Rogers, and Ralph Tryon, 1997, "Evaluating International Economic Policy with the Federal Reserve's Global Model," *Federal Reserve Bulletin* (Washington: Federal Reserve), pp. 797–817.

Lipsey, R.G., 1960, "The Relation Between Unemployment and the Rate of Change of Money Wage Rates in the United Kingdom 1862–1957: A Further Analysis," *Economica,* new series, Vol. 27 (February), pp. 1–31.

Lucas, Robert E., Jr., 1967, "Adjustment Costs and the Theory of Supply," *Journal of Political Economy,* Vol. 75 (August), pp. 321–34.

———, 1972, "Expectations and the Neutrality of Money," *Journal of Economic Theory,* Vol. 4 (April), pp. 103–24.

———, 1976, "Econometric Policy Evaluation: A Critique," in *The Phillips Curve and Labor Markets,* ed. by Karl Brunner and Allan H. Meltzer, Carnegie-Rochester Conference Series on Public Policy, Vol. 1 (Amsterdam: North-Holland).

———, 1988, "On the Mechanics of Economic Development," *Journal of Monetary Economics,* Vol. 22 (July), pp. 3–42.

Ludvigson, Sydney, 1996, "The Macroeconomic Effects of Government Debt in a Stochastic Growth Model," *Journal of Monetary Economics,* Vol. 38 (August), pp. 24–45.

Macklem, Tiff, 1996, "Asymmetry in the Monetary Transmission Mechanism: What Can We Learn From VARS?" (unpublished; Ottawa: Bank of Canada).

———, David Rose, and Robert Tetlow, 1995, "Government Debt and Deficits in Canada: A Macro Simulation Analysis," Working Paper 95-4 (Ottawa: Bank of Canada).

Mankiw, N. Gregory, 1988, "Comment" on De Long and Summers, *Brookings Papers on Economic Activity: 2,* Brookings Institution, pp. 481–85.

Masson, Paul R., 1987, "The Dynamics of a Two-Country Minimodel Under Rational Expectations," *Annales d'Economie et de Statistique,* pp. 37–69.

———, Steven Symansky, Richard Haas, and Michael Dooley, 1988, "MULTIMOD: A Multi-Region Econometric Model," *Staff Studies for the World Economic Outlook* (Washington: International Monetary Fund, July), pp. 50–104.

Masson, Paul R., and Steven Symansky, 1992, "Evaluating the EMS and EMU Using Stochastic Simulations," in *Macroeconomic Policy Coordination in Europe: The ERM and Monetary Union,* ed. by Ray Barrell and John Whitley (London: Sage Publications).

———, and Guy Meredith, 1990, *MULTIMOD MARK II: A Revised and Extended Model,* IMF Occasional Paper No. 71 (Washington: International Monetary Fund).

Masson, Paul R., and Bart G. Turtelboom, 1997, "Characteristics of the Euro, the Demand for Reserves, and Policy Coordination Under EMU," in *EMU and the International Monetary System,* ed. by P. Masson, T. Krueger, and B. Turtelboom (Washington: International Monetary Fund).

McDonald, Ian M., 1997, "The Australian Inflation Target and the Shape of the Short-Run Phillips Curve" (unpublished; Melbourne, Australia: University of Melbourne).

McGuirk, Anne Kenny, 1987, "Measuring Price Competitiveness for Industrial Country Trade in Manufactures," IMF Working Paper 87/34 (Washington: International Monetary Fund).

McKibbin, W.J., and J.D. Sachs, 1991, *Global Linkages: Macroeconomic Interdependence and Cooperation in the World Economy* (Washington: Brookings Institution).

Meredith, Guy, 1989, "INTERMOD 2.0: Model Specification and Simulation Properties," Working Paper 89-7 (Ottawa, Canada: Working Group on International Macroeconomics, Department of Finance).

———, 1991, "Changes to MULTIMOD Since the July 1990 IMF Occasional Paper No. 71" (unpublished; Washington: International Monetary Fund).

———, 1997, "Competitiveness Weights in MULTIMOD" (unpublished; Washington: International Monetary Fund).

Patterson, Kerry D. and Bahram Pesaran, 1992, "Intertemporal Elasticity of Substitution Consumption in the United States and the United Kingdom," *Review of Economics and Statistics,* Vol. 74 (November), pp. 573–84.

Persson, Torsten, 1985, "Deficits and Intergenerational Welfare in Open Economies," *Journal of International Economics,* Vol. 19 (August), pp. 67–84.

Phillips, A.W., 1958, "The Relation Between Unemployment and the Rate of Change of Money Wage Rates in the United Kingdom, 1861–1957," *Economica,* Vol. 25 (November), pp. 283–99.

Ricketts, Nicholas, and David Rose, 1995, "Inflation, Learning, and Monetary Policy Regimes in the G-7 Economies," Working Paper 95-6 (Ottawa: Bank of Canada).

Romer, Christina, and David Romer, 1989, "Does Monetary Policy Matter? A New Test in the Spirit of Friedman and Schwartz," in *NBER Macroeconomics Annual,* ed. by O. Blanchard and S. Fischer (Cambridge, Massachusetts; London, United Kingdom: MIT Press).

Romer, Paul M., 1990, "Endogenous Technological Change," *Journal of Political Economy,* Vol. 98 (October), pp. S71–S102.

Saint-Paul, Gilles, 1992, "Fiscal Policy in an Endogenous Growth Model," *Quarterly Journal of Economics,* Vol. 107 (November), pp. 1243–59.

Seater, John T., 1993, "Ricardian Equivalence," *Journal of Economic Literature,* Vol. 31 (March), pp. 142–90.

Summers, Lawrence H., 1981, "Taxation and Corporate Investment: a *q*-Theory Approach," *Brookings Papers on Economic Activity: 1,* Brookings Institution, pp. 67–127.

———, 1988, "Should Keynesian Economics Dispense with the Phillips Curve?" in *Unemployment, Hysteresis and the Natural Rate Hypothesis,* ed. by Rod Cross (Oxford, United Kingdom; New York: Blackwell).

Tanzi, Vito, and Domenico Fanizza, 1995, "Fiscal Deficits and Public Debt in Industrial Countries, 1970–1994," IMF Working Paper 95/49 (Washington: International Monetary Fund).

Taylor, John, 1980, "Aggregate Dynamics and Staggered Contracts," *Journal of Political Economy,* Vol. 88 (February), pp. 1–23.

———, 1993, "Discretion Versus Policy Rules in Practice," Carnegie-Rochester Conference Series on Public Policy, Vol. 39 (December), pp. 195–220.

———, 1996, "How Should Monetary Policy Respond to Shocks While Maintaining Long-Run Price Stability?—Conceptual Issues," in *Achieving Price Stability: A Symposium* (Kansas City, Missouri: Federal Reserve Bank of Kansas City).

Tobin, James, 1969, "A General Equilibrium Approach to Monetary Theory," *Journal of Money, Credit and Banking,* Vol. 1 (February), pp. 15–29.

Treadway, Arthur B., 1969, "On Rational Entrepreneurial Behaviour and the Demand for Investment," *Review of Economic Studies,* Vol. 36 (April), pp. 227–40.

Turner, David, 1995, "Speed Limit and Asymmetric Effects from the Output Gap in the Seven Major Countries," *OECD Economic Studies,* Vol. 24 (1995/I), pp. 57–88.

Turnovsky, Stephen, 1996, "Fiscal Policy, Growth, and Macroeconomic Performance in a Small Open Economy," *Journal of International Economics,* Vol. 40, pp. 41–66.

Weil, Philippe, 1989, "Overlapping Families of Infinitely-Lived Agents," *Journal of Public Economics,* Vol. 38 (March), pp. 183–98.

Yaari, Menahem E., 1965, "Uncertain Lifetime, Life Insurance, and the Theory of the Consumer," *Review of Economic Studies,* Vol. 32 (January), pp. 137–50.

Zanello, Alessandro, and Dominique Desruelle, 1997, "A Primer on the IMF's Information Notice System," IMF Working Paper 97/71 (Washington: International Monetary Fund).

Recent Occasional Papers of the International Monetary Fund

139. Reinvigorating Growth in Developing Countries: Lessons from Adjustment Policies in Eight Economies, by David Goldsbrough, Sharmini Coorey, Louis Dicks-Mireaux, Balazs Horvath, Kalpana Kochhar, Mauro Mecagni, Erik Offerdal, and Jianping Zhou. 1996.

138. Aftermath of the CFA Franc Devaluation, by Jean A.P. Clément, with Johannes Mueller, Stéphane Cossé, and Jean Le Dem. 1996.

137. The Lao People's Democratic Republic: Systemic Transformation and Adjustment, edited by Ichiro Otani and Chi Do Pham. 1996.

136. Jordan: Strategy for Adjustment and Growth, edited by Edouard Maciejewski and Ahsan Mansur. 1996.

135. Vietnam: Transition to a Market Economy, by John R. Dodsworth, Erich Spitäller, Michael Braulke, Keon Hyok Lee, Kenneth Miranda, Christian Mulder, Hisanobu Shishido, and Krishna Srinivasan. 1996.

134. India: Economic Reform and Growth, by Ajai Chopra, Charles Collyns, Richard Hemming, and Karen Parker with Woosik Chu and Oliver Fratzscher. 1995.

133. Policy Experiences and Issues in the Baltics, Russia, and Other Countries of the Former Soviet Union, edited by Daniel A. Citrin and Ashok K. Lahiri. 1995.

132. Financial Fragilities in Latin America: The 1980s and 1990s, by Liliana Rojas-Suárez and Steven R. Weisbrod. 1995.

131. Capital Account Convertibility: Review of Experience and Implications for IMF Policies, by staff teams headed by Peter J. Quirk and Owen Evans. 1995.

130. Challenges to the Swedish Welfare State, by Desmond Lachman, Adam Bennett, John H. Green, Robert Hagemann, and Ramana Ramaswamy. 1995.

129. IMF Conditionality: Experience Under Stand-By and Extended Arrangements. Part II: Background Papers. Susan Schadler, Editor, with Adam Bennett, Maria Carkovic, Louis Dicks-Mireaux, Mauro Mecagni, James H.J. Morsink, and Miguel A. Savastano. 1995.

128. IMF Conditionality: Experience Under Stand-By and Extended Arrangements. Part I: Key Issues and Findings, by Susan Schadler, Adam Bennett, Maria Carkovic, Louis Dicks-Mireaux, Mauro Mecagni, James H.J. Morsink, and Miguel A. Savastano. 1995.

127. Road Maps of the Transition: The Baltics, the Czech Republic, Hungary, and Russia, by Biswajit Banerjee, Vincent Koen, Thomas Krueger, Mark S. Lutz, Michael Marrese, and Tapio O. Saavalainen. 1995.

126. The Adoption of Indirect Instruments of Monetary Policy, by a staff team headed by William E. Alexander, Tomás J.T. Baliño, and Charles Enoch. 1995.

125. United Germany: The First Five Years—Performance and Policy Issues, by Robert Corker, Robert A. Feldman, Karl Habermeier, Hari Vittas, and Tessa van der Willigen. 1995.

124. Saving Behavior and the Asset Price "Bubble" in Japan: Analytical Studies, edited by Ulrich Baumgartner and Guy Meredith. 1995.

123. Comprehensive Tax Reform: The Colombian Experience, edited by Parthasarathi Shome. 1995.

122. Capital Flows in the APEC Region, edited by Mohsin S. Khan and Carmen M. Reinhart. 1995.

121. Uganda: Adjustment with Growth, 1987–94, by Robert L. Sharer, Hema R. De Zoysa, and Calvin A. McDonald. 1995.

120. Economic Dislocation and Recovery in Lebanon, by Sena Eken, Paul Cashin, S. Nuri Erbas, Jose Martelino, and Adnan Mazarei. 1995.

119. Singapore: A Case Study in Rapid Development, edited by Kenneth Bercuson with a staff team comprising Robert G. Carling, Aasim M. Husain, Thomas Rumbaugh, and Rachel van Elkan. 1995.

118. Sub-Saharan Africa: Growth, Savings, and Investment, by Michael T. Hadjimichael, Dhaneshwar Ghura, Martin Mühleisen, Roger Nord, and E. Murat Uçer. 1995.

Note: For information on the title and availability of Occasional Papers not listed, please consult the IMF Publications Catalog or contact IMF Publication Services.